Tax Guide 403

FAMILY TRUSTS & TRUSTORS

by

Holmes F. Crouch
Tax Specialist

Published by

Allyear Tax Guides

**20484 Glen Brae Drive
Saratoga, CA 95070**

ISBN 0-944817-61-0

LCCN 2001 130375

Printed in U.S.A.

Series 400
Owners & Sellers

Tax Guide 403

FAMILY TRUSTS & TRUSTORS

For other titles in print, see page 224.

The author: **Holmes F. Crouch**
For more about the author, see page 221.

PREFACE

If you are a knowledge-seeking **taxpayer** looking for information, this book can be helpful to you. It is designed to be read — from cover to cover — in about eight hours. Or, it can be "skim-read" in about 30 minutes.

Either way, you are treated to **tax knowledge** . . . *beyond the ordinary*. The "beyond" is that which cannot be found in IRS publications, FedWorld on-line services, tax software programs, Internet chatrooms, or e-mail bulletins.

Taxpayers have different levels of interest in a selected subject. For this reason, this book starts with introductory fundamentals and progresses onward. You can verify the progression by chapter and section in the table of contents. In the text, "applicable law" is quoted in pertinent part. Key phrases and key tax forms are emphasized. Real-life examples are given . . . in down-to-earth style.

This book has 12 chapters. This number provides depth without cross-subject rambling. Each chapter starts with a head summary of meaningful information.

To aid in your skim-reading, informative diagrams and tables are placed strategically throughout the text. By leafing through page by page, reading the summaries and section headings, and glancing at the diagrams and tables, you can get a good handle on the matters covered.

Effort has been made to update and incorporate all of the latest tax law changes that are *significant* to the title subject. However, "beyond the ordinary" does not encompass every conceivable variant of fact and law that might give rise to protracted dispute and litigation. Consequently, if a particular statement or paragraph is crucial to your own specific case, you are urged to seek professional counseling. Otherwise, the information presented is general and is designed for a broad range of reader interests.

The Author

INTRODUCTION

A trustor is a natural person who has acquired property interests of value during his or her wealth-building years. Having done so, there comes a time when arrangements are made for transferring gratuitously those property interests to family members and others down generational lines. This is the pre-stage for the creation of a family trust. At this point, a trustor is variously called: *transferor* (of property interests), *creator* (of a trust with property), or *grantor* (of reversionary interests in trust property).

There is more — much, much more — to family trusts than conferring with an attorney in a prestigious legal firm which prepares a 35-page (plus or minus) legal document under a state's trust law. There's a whole separate world of *federal* transfer taxation, trust administration, and income taxation out there. These matters do not come to light until after the first property interest of value is transferred **irrevocably** into the trust. Said event may not occur for 5, 10, or 20 years after the trust instrument is prepared.

Consequently, the general procedure is to read only pages 1, 2, and 3 of a trust instrument. This is where the distributive intent is stated, and where the names of trustees and beneficiaries are spelled out. The rest of the 35-page tome is too intimidating to ask what the legalese and contingency clauses are all about. In desperation, the document is signed . . . with a prayer and a hope.

We think we can improve on the situation above. We will do so by previewing with you what others can only post view, after your demise. We believe we can do this by telling you about the working components of a trust, the "why" of transfer taxation, the tax returns required, life estates for surviving spouses, the role of charitable remainders, and the special valuation rules for appreciated property, family farms and businesses, and other family wealth. We present these matters in the context of—

☐ Abusive Family Trusts
☐ Ordinary Family Trusts, and
☐ Generation-Skipping Trusts

Abusive family trusts are those in which the transferable property interests are not fully vested in the trust entity. No transfer tax is computed and paid, nor is such tax ever expected to be paid. The so-called "trust" conveys the illusion of validity via interlocking corporate and partnership arrangements whose objective is pure tax avoidance. There are anti-abuse rules against these kinds of trusts.

Ordinary family trusts are those in which the transfer of property has been validated. All gift and death tax returns have been filed (or will be filed), and the trustees are prudent and diligent. For focusing purposes, we consider ordinary family trusts to have potential assets in the range of 3 million to 10 million dollars. This is the domain of what we class as "modest wealth" families.

Generation-skipping trusts are especially attractive for above-modest-wealth families: those in the 10 million to 100 million dollar range. The chief attraction is a $1,000,000 (inflation adjusted) **exemption** PER TRUSTOR for skipping over children and transferring property interests directly to grandchildren, great-grandchildren, and perhaps great-great-grandchildren. The beauty of the exemption is that, if it is expressly allocated in the trust instrument by property description and distributee name, any long-term appreciation of that property's value is exempt from the GST tax. The GST tax is a flat 55% rate times the non-exempt value of the property transferred. All property in a GST trust must either vest or terminate within 90 years of creating such a trust.

Knowing what is likely to take place with your property interests after your death should help you prepare a better trust instrument before your death. This is the premise throughout this book. Where plausible, we give you specific examples of what we mean. Test us, if you wish, by jumping ahead and reading Chapter 8: Desirable Trust Features. Then go back and read — or skim read — all of our chapters.

In the end, we think you will acquire with this book the necessary knowledge to take a more decisive hand in clarifying the fine points and intentions of your trust. If you do not do so while alive, the "professionals" will take over after your demise. Not only will they deplete your assets, they will exasperate your family trustee and beneficiaries and cause you great pain after life.

CONTENTS

1

INTRODUCTORY ASPECTS

When Properly Created And Funded, A Trust Is
a Valid Entity For Estate Planning. The
Greater The Wealth In A Family, The More
Useful A Trust Becomes. Wealth, However,
Often Leads To Abusive Trust Practices Which
Can Render The Arrangement Being Taxed As A
Corporation Rather Than As a Distribution
Conduit. The Person Having The Most Say
Over The Trust Creation Is Its TRUSTOR.
He/She Holds Ownership To Property Which Is
Gratuitously Dedicated Into Trust For Its
Enjoyment By Others. Although Created Under
State Law, Trusts Are Tax Policed Under
Federal Law: The "Internal Revenue Code."

A trust is a legal entity created under state law. As such, it
becomes an enforceable contract between a trustor (creator) and a
trustee (manager) for qualified trust property. The purpose of the
contract — called: *trust instrument* — is to conserve, rearrange,
manage, and **distribute** trust property (its corpus principal) to
designated beneficiaries over (usually) extended periods of time.

The types of beneficiaries on whom we focus are members of a
family. Said members are grandparents, parents, children,
grandchildren, and the spouses and siblings thereof. Also included
may be one or more designated charities. The income and principal
of the trust are distributed to those persons gratuitously. This means
that the recipients of the gratuities provide no services or
compensation to the trust for any money or property they receive.
They pay tax on the income received, but not on the principal.

The legal owner of the property in trust before it is distributed is the trust entity itself. This presumes that the transfer of property from the trustor to the trust is irrevocable. That is, the trustor has severed all dominion and control over the trust property. Such severance is signified when, and only when, all (fair market) valuation accounting for the property has been made, and all applicable transfer taxes paid.

In this, our introductory chapter, therefore, we want to review the fundamental features of a trust entity, and provide instructive pointers to those trustors whose property either already has been, or is intended to be, conveyed into trust. Our position is that a trustor should be his own man (or her own woman) and not be dissuaded by prestigious trust promoters and preparers. There are federal tax rules out there of which trust preparers themselves are often unaware. Where there is modest or above-modest family wealth involved, abusive trust practices take on an aura and mystique of their own. All we can do here is call to your attention some of those practices and point out the more proper courses of action to take.

Meaning of "Trustor"

You will not find the word "trustor" in any ordinary college dictionary. The nearest you will find is the word "trust." At the end of nearly 280 definitive words describing a trust, the words *trustable (adj.)* and *truster (n.)* are tacked on. Otherwise, you are left dangling.

However, if you will look in a dictionary of legal terms, you will find trustor defined as—

One who creates a trust; more often called the settlor.

In the same legal dictionary, you will find settlor defined as—

Donor; Trustor. *One who creates a trust by giving real and personal property in trust to another (the trustee) for the benefit of a third person (the beneficiary). One who gives such property is said to settle it on, or bring title to rest with, the trustee.*

A related synonymous term is the word *grantor*. A grantor is defined as—

*One who gives, allows, or transfers something to another without compensation; especially a gift of land made by the one having authority over it. The one giving the gift or making the transfer is the **grantor**. The recipient is the **grantee**.*

Similarly synonymous to trustor is the word *transferor*. A transferor is defined as—

*One who conveys or removes from one person to another; one who sells or gives; specifically one who takes over possession or control as in the transfer of title to land. The recipient of something transferred is the **transferee**.*

Altogether, now, the "trustor" means one who owns property, who gives, grants, transfers, or settles it in trust for someone called "a beneficiary." In family trust arrangements it is more common to provide for multiple beneficiaries. To legalize the arrangement, the giving, granting, transferring must be in accordance with state law where the trustor or his property is domiciled. Once prepared under a particular state law, that state retains its original jurisdiction over the trust, even though the trustor may move to a different state.

State Law Provisions

Every state where a potential trustor is domiciled has its own trust law. Said law is found in the Probate Code for that state. You do not have to be an attorney to access the probate code for your state. Simply visit the legal section of your local public library, or visit the county law library nearest you. County law libraries are tax-exempt entities. As such, they must allow public access if they wish to continue their tax-exempt status. Visit said library and locate a "compact edition" of said code. Browse through it for an hour or two at least. Don't try to study it. Just browse, looking for sections that attract your attention in a common sense way. If you are intrigued by a particular section, photocopy it for perusal later.

In the California Probate Code, for example, Trust Law is found in the section headed: *Creation, Validity, Modification, and Termination of Trusts.* A few excerpts from this volume are helpful in recognizing the key legal characteristics of a valid trust.

Selected excerpts (with section numbers) are:

1. *A trust is created only if the settlor [trustor]* ***properly manifests*** *an intention to create a trust.* [¶ 15201]

2. *A trust is created* ***only if there is trust property.*** [¶ 15202]

3. *A trust may be created for any purpose that is not illegal or against public policy.* [¶ 15203]

4. *A trust . . . is created* ***only of there is a beneficiary.*** *This requirement is satisfied if the trust instrument provides for either of the following:*

   (a) A beneficiary or class of beneficiaries that is ascertainable with reasonable certainty or that is sufficiently described so it can be determined that some person meets the description or is within the class.

   (b) A grant of a power to the trustee or some other person to select the beneficiaries based on a standard or in the discretion of the trustee or other person. [¶ 15205]

5. *If the trust instrument provides that a beneficiary's interest in* ***income*** *is not subject to voluntary or involuntary transfer, the beneficiary's interest in income under the trust may not be transferred and is not subject to enforcement of a money judgment until paid to the beneficiary.* [¶ 15300]

6. *If the trust instrument provides that a beneficiary's interest in* ***principal*** *[corpus] is not subject to voluntary or involuntary transfer, the beneficiary's interest in principal may not be transferred and is not subject to enforcement of a money judgment until paid to the beneficiary.* [¶ 15301]

7. *Unless a trust instrument is expressly made irrevocable by the trust instrument, the trust is revocable by the settlor. This applies only where the settlor is domiciled in this state when the trust is created, where the trust instrument is executed in this state, or where the trust instrument provides that the law of this state governs the trust.* [¶ 15400]

8. *If all beneficiaries of an irrevocable trust consent, they may compel modification or termination of the trust upon petition to the* [probate] *court.* [¶ 15403]

9. *A trust terminates when any of the following occurs:*

   (a)   The term of the trust expires.
   (b)   The trust purpose is fulfilled.
   (c)   The trust purpose becomes unlawful.
   (d)   The trust purpose becomes impossible to fulfill.
   (e)   The trust is revoked. [¶ 15407]

10. *The statutory rule against perpetuities . . . seeks to disallow . . . any interest or trust beyond . . . the expiration of a period of time not exceeding 21 years after the death of the survivor of specified lives in being at the creation of the trust or other property arrangement.* [¶ 21209]

The Working Components

With state law as background, it is instructive to identify those day-to-day components that make up a trust . . . and make it work. A trust is more than just a legal contract on paper. It is a body of property, people, and law.

There are at least eight features — or primary components — which make a trust work. In synopsis form, these eight components are:

1. TRUSTOR — the creator of the trust and the transferor of designated property thereinto. The trustor must own the property that he transfers into trust.

2. TRUST INSTRUMENT — the agreement, declaration, contract, or other legal document prepared in accordance with applicable state law.

3. TRUST LAW — the probate code of the state of domicile of the trustor **and** of the state of situs of out-state real and tangible property; trust law is identified by its own section in the probate code with such title words as: *Creation, Validity, Modification, and Termination of Trusts.*

4. TRUST PROPERTY — specific property assignments either predesignated by Exhibit A of a living trust, by irrevocable transfers while the trustor is alive, or by testamentary transfers in a will at time of the trustor's death. Once irrevocably assigned, the trust entity is the *legal owner* of the property therein.

5. TRUSTEE — the *manager* of the trust property pursuant to instructions to him enumerated in the trust instrument; as said manager, he is entitled to a trustee fee.

6. BENEFICIARIES — one or more living human beings and specified generational unborns of existing human beings; these persons are the *beneficial owners* (but not economic owners) of the trust property.

7. CHARITIES — qualified tax-exempt organizations specifically designated by will or the trust, or as selected by the trustee where such discretionary powers are granted by the trustor.

8. PROBATE COURT — the judicial process for resolving any disputes and claims by creditors, beneficiaries, state authorities, and charities; probate jurisdiction is limited to ownership matters, beneficial rights, and trustee malfeasance. Probate courts have no jurisdiction over federal tax matters.

As a summary of the above "working components" of a trust, we present Figure 1.1. Not all trusts provide for charities; there is no requirement that they do so. A charity can be thought of as a contingent or remainder beneficiary for reducing taxes and closing out the remnants of a trust upon its termination.

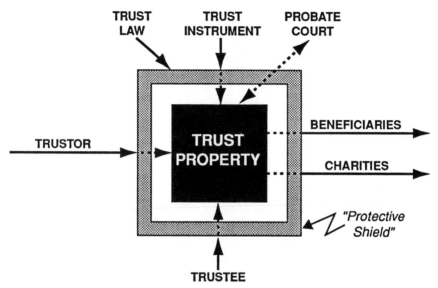

Fig.1.1 - The Essential "Components" of a Viable Trust

As depicted in Figure 1.1, the most practical way of visualizing a trust is to think of it as a warehouse for the storage of property. The warehouse walls (labeled "protective shield" in Figure 1.1) are the trust law of the state where the trustor and property are domiciled. Once the warehouse is filled and locked, specific procedures must be pursued for removing the property and distributing it, one piece at a time. The procedures for doing so are addressed in the trust instrument.

Trust Instrument: General Contents

The glue that holds property in trust together is the trust instrument. The term "instrument" means any enforceable written agreement between two or more persons: trustor, trustee, beneficiaries, and (possibly) others. The instrument should contain matters of substance only. Ideally, it should be — but seldom is — devoid of legal puffery and boilerplate.

Certain key elements must be included in a trust instrument before it is legally enforceable. Among the more common content requirements are the following:

1. The name of the trustor and a declaration of his creative intent. This is usually set forth in a preamble statement.

2. The name and domicile of the trust entity, with specific reference to the law of which state shall apply.

3. A description of the specific property intended to be dedicated irrevocably to the trust entity.

4. A specific clarification of the trustor's ownership interest in property (and title form) where there is more than one owner of that property. This is particularly important for community property, joint tenancy property, tenants by entirety property, tenants in common property, and co-ownership of ongoing businesses.

5. A description of the contemplated use of the property for the generation of income and capital for distribution to beneficiaries.

6. The name and status of each beneficiary and successor beneficiary, and his/her relationship to the trustor.

7. The appointment of an initial trustee and successor trustees, by name and domicile of each. The practice of appointing co-trustees is discouraged where there are possible conflicts in management style and accounting discipline.

8. A description of the powers, duties, and liabilities of the trustee, with a "hold harmless" clause for management errors and losses when acting in good faith.

9. A procreational clause indicating the specific generational sequence of beneficiaries to be serviced by the trust. Except for the first generation of beneficiaries where death is the cutoff for distributions, successive generational cutoffs should be based upon attaining a specific age.

10. A clearly defined termination clause, directing when and how the trust shall be terminated. Without this clause, a trust runs the risk of being taxed as a corporation, rather than as a trust.

Of all the content requirements above, the keymost desirable features of a trust instrument are its clarity and specificity. These characteristics comprise the mechanism — the heart and lifebeat, if you will — that makes a trust work or not work. Unfortunately, most trust instruments are cluttered with endless contingencies, legal trivia, and quagmire clauses that work to thwart the best intentions of the trustor. Lack of clarity, readability, and comprehension are a shortcoming of all trusts.

The Trustor & His Property

Upon the creation of a trust, the one person who has greatest control over the content and clarity of a trust instrument is the trustor. He (or she) is the one who is paying for the services of a trust preparer (most often an attorney). A trustor should not be intimidated by attorneys or other preparers of his/her trust instrument. Each trustor should be independent minded to read, spot, and inquire about the boilerplate trivia and quagmire clauses that can invariably creep in. In other words, every trustor should be his own man (or own woman) when a trust instrument is initially prepared, subsequently amended, or significantly revised.

A trustor, first off, has to be a human being. He has to own property of value that can be useful to others after his demise. Here, the term "property" means any form of assets: real, tangible, and intangible — whether owned in his own right, in co-ownership with others, or aggregated into an ongoing business which he controls. A trustor also has to have someone whom he can trust to manage and care for his property once it is irrevocably assigned to his trust. Regardless of trust law legalese, he is not required to put all of his property in trust. There is a lot of clutter in every human being's estate which is best left out of the trust.

The role of a trustor is defined more by the kind and value of property than by any other single factor. If he has property co-owned with others, his percentage of ownership interest must be clearly ascertainable in one or more evidentiary documents. By "property of value," we mean that which has *significant market value*. By "significant value," we mean property which is coveted by someone else to the point that the trustor would fight to protect his ownership interests. After all, if you put an old pair of shoes in a trust, who really cares? But if you put a parcel of waterfront land in trust, there would be many persons and entities in the public domain would covet that property for their own uses.

A trustor, therefore, is a person who owns property of value, and who goes through the steps necessary to create a trust of it. Stated differently, a trustor is any person who owns or has power over the use of property, who wants to dedicate it to a trust for use and consumption by one or more other persons: his beneficiaries. Without property of value, there can be no real trust.

As you can sense from our depiction in Figure 1.1, the core feature of a trust is the property that is dedicated to it. Primarily, it should be income producing and capable of being partitioned into "small slices" for distribution of corpus (or capital) as needed. Here, we use the term "property" in its broadest and most generalized sense. The reason we do so is that there is no statutory limitation on the specific type of property that can be transferred into trust. As long as the property is not illegally obtained, and its intended use is not violative of public policy, there are no statutory prohibitions against the type of property assigned to a trust.

Once an item of property is in trust irrevocably, the trust becomes a valid, viable, and operating entity of its own. It is not necessary, however, that all items of property of the trustor be dedicated to a trust at the same time. He can assign some in trust during life, and other items can be assigned after death. Whenever assigned, the property can be rearranged by the trustee for more efficient administration purposes..

Meaning of "Power of Appointment"

One of the most dangerous and least understood features of trust activities is the term "power of appointment." The term applies to the power of any person having a financial interest in the trust to **appoint/take** unto himself any part of the trust property. The taking/appointing of property refers to the trust corpus or principal only. It does not refer to the periodic income of the trust which is used to pay legitimate expenses and debts, and proper distributions.

It is the invasion of the corpus or principal that can sap the vitality and credibility of a trust.

There are four categories of persons who have a financial interest in a trust. These are: (1) trustors, (2) trustees, (3) beneficiaries, and (4) trust preparers. Lenders, borrowers, creditors, suppliers, or other persons or entities engaged in ordinary business transactions with a trust are not "financial interests" (in the beneficial sense). They have customary legal rights outside of the trust instrument for recovering their costs of goods and services rendered to the trust, or to any of its financial interests.

A power of appointment slips in the trust instrument sometimes inadvertently, and sometimes surreptitiously. The trustor and his preparer try to be too clever. They seek to cover every conceivable contingency in the distant future that might require special access to the trust property. They thereby insert various contingency clauses interpretable as powers of appointment. It is not that powers of appointment are never allowed. It is just that any appointive power must be restricted, constrained, and limited to a specific purpose involving unusual circumstances.

For example, as a trust beneficiary, a surviving spouse or handicapped child of the trustor may be granted a *limited* power of appointment. Such power authorizes invasion of the trust corpus for such contingencies as—

(1) Continuing his/her customary support.
(2) Defraying major medical and hospital expenses.
(3) Meeting special education and rehabilitation needs.
(4) Addressing unexpected financial hardships.

Where no special circumstances are prescribed for access to the trust corpus, and there are clauses that imply any power of appointment, said power is construed to be a general power. Examples of implied general power include: (a) reversionary interests of the trustor; (b) trustee discretion much too broad; (c) intercession on behalf of one or more beneficiaries, and (d) pledging any part of the trust corpus to nonbeneficiaries. Any general power of appointment can defeat the purpose of a trust and deplete its assets prematurely.

So dangerous is the power of appointment concept to the vitality of a trust that we feel compelled to present a depiction of it. Accordingly, we present Figure 1.2. The point that we want to get across is that, if you are a trustor, you must exercise great care to prevent any general powers of appointment from creeping into your trust documentation.

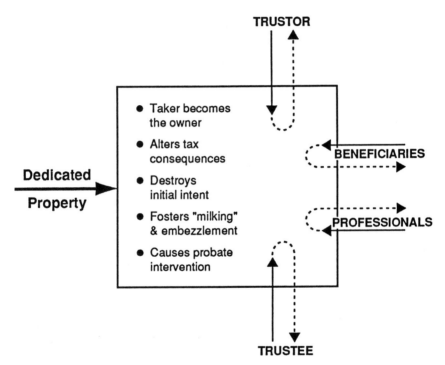

Fig.1.2 - Power of Appointment Dangers in a Trust

Beware of Abusive Trusts

The prospect of creating a family trust is the darling of estate planners and trust promoters. They portray such a trust as a unique tax shelter and wealth secreter. They arrange matters in such a way that the trustor, his spouse, his children, and his grandchildren can borrow against the trust property, split up its income, and slice up its corpus property to defray family living expenses, educational needs, recreational activities, and business obligations. This is all done under the mystique and magic of a trust arrangement which is private, tax-free, and nonaccountable. When any such arrangement is "too good to be true," beware!

Although a trust is formed under state law, it is policed under federal law. No matter how cleverly contrived, an irrevocable family trust is a TAX ACCOUNTABLE entity. The federal agency having the greatest oversight in this respect — as you surely already know — is the Internal Revenue Service (IRS). The IRS has issued a stern warning [Notice 97-24] to trust preparers and promoters not to engage in abusive trust practices.

As described in IRS Notice 97-24, an abusive trust attempts to hide the true ownership of its assets, and purports to provide special tax benefits without any meaningful change in the trustor's dominion and control over those assets. The ownership arrangement is camouflaged through a series of interlocking trusts (business, residential, charitable, and foreign). Each trust has a different beneficiary. Funds are transferred from one trust to another based on vague exchange agreements, rental leasebacks, service contracts, charitable gifts, and other distributive nuances. The net result is that no assets are transfer taxed (as they would be if all dominion and control were given up) and no perceptible taxable income is generated. The entire arrangement is a sham. Tax **evasion** is clearly the motivation.

We present in Figure 1.3 the key distinguishing features between a valid trust and a sham trust.

For a family trust to be tax legal, all transfer taxes — gift, estate, generation-skipping — must be assessed and paid. Said taxes are imposed on the privilege of transferring gratuitously assets from a trustor to his successors, heirs, and assigns. Until all applicable taxes are paid, any purported trust entity is not recognized by the IRS. We devote all of Chapter 2 to these matters: Imposition of Transfer Tax.

Definitions re "Family"

As the title of this book implies, our primary focus is on family trusts. As such, we have to define what a "family" is, and who constitutes legitimate members of the family. For such a definition,

1	**2**	**3**	**4**	**5**
Economic Owner	Dedication into Trust	Transfer Taxation	Powers of Appointment	Beneficial Rights
GENUINE TRUSTOR	Single Document	• Gift tax • Death Tax • GST Tax	Limited to Corpus Only	Exclusive up to Terminating Event
AGGRESSIVE TRUSTOR	Multiple Documents	Ingenious Bypass Schemes	General. Whatever, Whenever, Convenient	Frequently Interrupted and Rescinded

All Features of a Sham Arrangement

Fig. 1.3 - Transfer Tax: Proof of a Valid Trust

we look to IRC Section 2704(c): *Definitions and Special Rules.* Included in this tax code subsection are three paragraphs, namely:

(1) *Control* [by applicable family member],
(2) *Member of the Family*, and
(3) *Attribution* [treatment as belonging to].

Paragraph (1) of Section 2704(c) defines the term "control" as that exercised by—

an applicable family member [who is] *any lineal descendant of any parent of the transferor* [trustor] *or the transferor's spouse.*

A "parent of the transferor" is an ascendant of the trustor who creates the family trust.

Paragraph (2) of Section 2704(c) defines the term "member of the family" as—

with respect to any individual—

(A) such individual's spouse,

(B)   any ancestor or lineal descendant of such individual or such individual's spouse,
(C)   any brother or sister of the individual, and
(D)   any spouse of any individual described in (B) or (C).

Paragraph (3) of Section 2704(c) states that—

The rule of section 2701(e)(3) shall apply for determining the [ownership] interests held by any individual.

Section 2701(e)(3) is titled: ***Attribution of Indirect Holdings and Transfers.*** This attribution section reads in full as—

An individual shall be treated as holding any interest to the extent such interest is held indirectly by such individual through a corporation, partnership, trust or other entity. If any individual is treated as holding any [ownership]interest by reason of the preceding sentence, any transfer which results in such interest being treated as no longer held by such individual shall be treated as a transfer of such interest.

In other words, if an individual (human being) has an ownership interest in a corporation, partnership, proprietorship, trust, or other entity (e.g., mutual fund), he cannot convey ownership gratuitously to a family member without there being a transfer tax imposed.

A Trust is Not a Business

One of the most difficult concepts to get across to trustors — and to trustees and beneficiaries — is that a trust is NOT a business entity. A business entity is an entrepreneurial activity which seeks to make a profit on a continuing and ongoing basis, without end. The profit is shared among the **economic owners** of the business. An "economic owner" is one who contributes capital (money and property) to the formation and operation of a business. A business is classed as a corporation, partnership, or proprietorship. A corporation pays dividends to its owners (stockholders); a partnership pays distributive shares to its members; and a proprietorship "pays" all net profit to the sole owner.

In contrast, the term "trust" as used in the Internal Revenue Code refers to an ordinary (gratuitous) trust. Such is one by which **particular property** (not the "pots and pans") is conveyed by will, deed, or declaration of the trustor into one or more trusts, for the exclusive benefit of named persons. The named persons (beneficiaries) contribute no capital whatsoever to the formation and operation of the trust entity. The obligation on the trustee is primarily that of protecting and conserving the trust property, collecting income, and distributing or holding it (including corpus property) as prescribed by the trust instrument.

IRS Regulation § 301.7701-4(a) defines an ordinary trust in about 180 words. We extract the following specific wordage from this regulation:

*Usually, the beneficiaries of such a trust do no more than accept the benefits thereof, and are not the voluntary planners or creators of the trust arrangement. . . . An arrangement will be treated as a trust . . . if it can be shown that the purpose . . . is to vest in trustees responsibility for the protection and conservation of property for beneficiaries who cannot share in the discharge of this responsibility and, therefore, **are not associates in a joint enterprise for the conduct of business for profit**.* [Emphasis added.]

The above regulation does not prohibit a trust from accepting a pre-existing business of the trustor whether in corporate, partnership, or proprietorship form. Ostensibly, the pre-existing business is to be protected and conserved solely for the benefit of specifically named persons. The protection/conservation aspects must not include the enticement or participation of other persons into a for-profit enterprise. If obvious effort is made to attract additional owners, whether economic or beneficial, the trust is IRS taxed as a corporation and not as a trust.

We summarize the distinctions above in Figure 1.4. If you digest and apply the distinctions depicted, a trust indeed becomes a very useful tool for family estate planning.

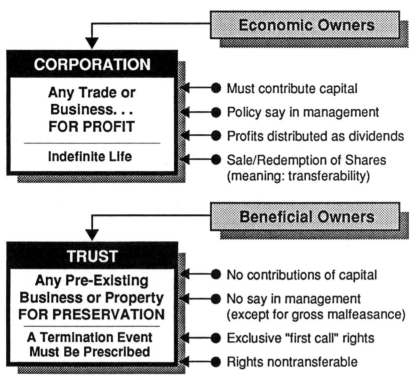

Fig. 1.4 - Key Distinctions Between a Corporation and a Trust

The "One Trust" Rule

The promotion of multiple trusts tends to be a fascination among financial planners, insurance agents, and covetous attorneys. They dream and scheme of circuitous arrangements of living trusts, split-interests trusts, reversionary trusts, charitable trusts, and foreign trusts. The promoters focus on enticing those whose individual trust estates *exceed* $3,000,000. In this domain of modest and above-modest wealth holders, there are some trustors who want to believe that the issues of transfer tax and income tax (with respect to trusts) can be avoided altogether.

Be informed now of IRC Section 643(f): *Treatment of Multiple Trusts*. This statutory mandate says—

For purposes of [the imposition of tax] . . . *2 or more trusts shall be treated as 1 trust if—*

(1)   such trusts have substantially the same grantor [trustor] *or grantors* [trustors] *and substantially the same primary beneficiary or beneficiaries, and*

(2)   a principal purpose of such trusts is the avoidance of the tax imposed by [the IR Code].

For purposes of the preceding sentence, a husband and a wife shall be treated as 1 person. [Emphasis added.]

Section 643(f) is called the "one trust" rule or, more technically, the *multiple trust aggregation* rule. This rule is the genesis of the IRS's authority to pursue abusive trust practices and put an end to them. The procedure for doing so is to classify the trusts as an "association" (of trustors, trustees, and beneficiaries) which is taxable as a corporation. This means that all property transactions are taxed as for-profit sales (rather than gratuitous transfers). And all income is treated as dividends which are double-taxed: once at the corporation level and again at the distributee level.

The regulations supporting Section 643(f) do soften the mandate somewhat. If each of two or more trusts have **substantially independent purposes** and tax avoidance is not the principal motivation for the arrangement, more than one trust may be allowed. A "substantially independent" purpose means separate economic groupings of beneficiaries by age, health, mental state, educational needs, long-term care, etc. Section 643(f) is intended to neither inhibit nor prohibit responsible estate planning based on genuine good cause.

2

IMPOSITION OF TRANSFER TAX

> There Are Three Specific Tax Laws That
> Impose A Transfer Tax, Namely: Sec. 2501 (re
> Gifts), 2001 (re Deaths), And 2601 (re GSTs:
> Generation-Skipping Transfers). The Gift And
> Death Taxes Are UNIFIED Into One Graduated
> Rate Schedule: 37% to 55%; The GST Tax Is
> Computed At the MAXIMUM Unified Rate of
> 55%. There Are Also a One-Time Unified
> Gift/Death EXCLUSION Up To $1,000,000 And
> A Separate GST Exemption, Before The
> Transfer Tax Is Known. Additionally, During
> Life, Gifts Are Encouraged By An "Annual" Per
> DONOR, Per DONEE Exclusion Which Is
> INDEPENDENT Of The Unified Amounts.

Transfer tax! "What is that?," you ask. If you pose this question to aggressive trust promoters, we doubt that you'll get a clear answer. You may even have to explain to them what your concept of a transfer tax is.

In as concise terms as possible, the *transfer tax* is a tax on the privilege of transferring property or money to others, gratuitously. There are applicable exclusions which can reduce the amount of tax.

The transfer concept goes back to the British Stamp Act of 1765 imposed on the American Colonies. It was a "stamp tax" on legal writs, newspaper ads, ships' bills of lading, and a wide variety of other transactions. It was a tax simply for authenticating a legal transfer of ownership from one person to another. Even today, there is a nominal "stamp tax" imposed by local county recorders on the transfer of title to real estate.

Another way of looking at the transfer tax is this. Suppose you paid $15,000 for a parcel of land and you sold it to some unrelated person for $100,000. When you receive the $100,000 you sign papers severing all ownership dominion and control over that parcel. In this example, you have an $85,000 capital gain (100,000 – 15,000). Is the $85,000 gain tax free? You surely know the answer.

Similarly, if you transfer a $100,000 item gratuitously to a member of your family (or into trust), would your severance of its ownership be tax free? If the transferee paid absolutely nothing for the item, would it still be tax free? No. And this is what annoys many trustors who want to pass their assets through to various members of their family.

In a nutshell, there are three forms of transfer taxes, namely: (1) gift tax (while donor/trustor is alive), (2) death tax (when the transferor/trustor deceases), and (3) generation-skipping tax (for skipping over children and transferring directly to grandchildren). Collectively, these taxes are called: *Estate and Gift Taxes*. There is a separate portion of the Internal Revenue Code that specifically addresses these taxes. Accordingly, in this chapter, we want to familiarize you with the three transfer taxes, when and how they are imposed, and the rates and exclusions that apply.

Tax Code Provisions

The Internal Revenue Code (IRC) has been officially designated by Congress as—

UNITED STATES CODE — TITLE 26

Within Title 26, there are eleven subtitles — A through K — which address various federal issues. The first three of these subtitles are:

Subtitle A — *Income Taxes*
Subtitle B — *Estate and Gift Taxes*
Subtitle C — *Employment Taxes*

Subtitle B is our focus; it consists of three chapters, namely:

Chapter 11 — Estate Tax • Sections 2001-2209

Chapter 12 — Gift Tax • Sections 2501-2524

Chapter 13 — Tax on Generation-Skipping Transfers
• Sections 2601–2663

Altogether, there are about 90 sections in the tax code that specifically address the imposition and computation of the transfer tax. In addition, there are penalty and collection enforcement sections which deal with willful attempts to avoid the transfer tax.

An example of the impediments to dodging the tax is Section 877: *Expatriation to Avoid Tax*. Because of the high rates applicable to transfer taxation, the setting up of foreign trusts and the expatriation of oneself and his money to a "tax haven" country is a fascinating consideration . . . at least in passing.

For expatriated wealth, subsection 877(a)(2): *Certain Individuals Treated as Having Tax Avoidance Purpose*, applies. The essence of this law is that, if an individual has *a net worth of $500,000 or more* at the time of giving up his U.S. citizenship—

> [He] *shall be treated as having a principal purpose the avoidance of taxes under subtitle B* [Estate and Gift Taxes]. . . . [T]*here is hereby imposed a tax of 30 percent of the* [expatriated] *amounts from . . . the U.S. . . . for the 10-year period immediately* [following] *the close of the taxable year . . .* [of the loss] *of U.S. citizenship.*

Section 877(a) is another way of telling you not to expect tax magic when creating exotic-sounding family trusts. If you will be patient and read through the transfer tax rules, digging for the exclusions and exceptions, we think you can work things out.

Transfers in General

What does the tax code say about gratuitous transfers? There are two specific sections that address the issue, definitively. One section pertains to gifts during the life of the donor/trustor: the other section pertains to transfers taking effect at (and after) death of the grantor/trustor. Both clearly intimate that the extent of gratuitousness (without or with compensation) is the very purpose of the transfer tax. These two transfer-specific rules are Section 2511 (re gifts) and Section 2043 (re death). First, let us examine Section 2511: *Transfers in General.*

Section 2511(a): *Scope*, reads in full as—

Subject to the limitations contained in [Chapter 12: Gift Tax], *the tax imposed by section 2501 **shall apply whether** the transfer is **in trust or otherwise**, whether the gift is **direct or indirect**, and whether the property is real or personal, tangible or intangible; but, in the case of a nonresident not a citizen of the U.S., shall apply to a transfer only if the property is situated within the U.S.* [Emphasis added.]

We don't see much wiggle room here; do you? The clause "shall apply whether" shuts out most of those ingenious schemes that you may have heard and dreamed about.

Additionally, we tell you that the gift tax is not imposed upon the receipt of property; it is not a sales tax; it is not a property tax. Nor is it conditioned upon the ability to identify the donee at the time of transfer (as in a vaguely worded trust). As a deliberate act of accountability, it is a transfer tax on property that constitutes a "gift."

A gift is a voluntary transfer (in any form or manner) of property (of any kind or nature) from one person to another without any consideration or compensation being paid therefor. The transfer is gratuitous: pure and simple.

As Figure 2.1 indicates, there are some obstacles that prevent the imposition of the gift tax. One is that the donor must be competent and understand the nature of his transfer. A second obstacle is that the intended property must be actually delivered to the donee, or to his agent or representative (or trust). A third obstacle is that the donee must accept the property transferred, and assume all dominion and control of it thereafter.

A promise to make a gift is not a gift. Even the execution of a trust instrument in itself will not constitute a gift. The property subject to such trust must *actually and legally* be transferred to the

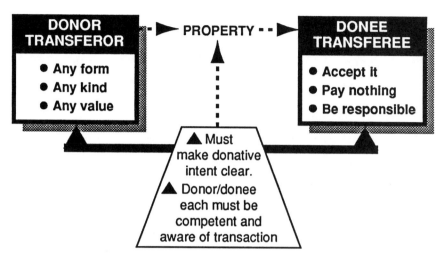

Fig. 2.1 - Fundamental Premise for the Taxing of Gratuitous Transfers

trust without any retention of powers by the donor, whatsoever. The transfer to trust, irrevocably, constitutes the delivery necessary to complete a gift. The term "irrevocably" means that the transfer tax has been computed and paid.

When Insufficient Consideration

The other transfer-specific tax law is Section 2043. Its title is: ***Transfers for Insufficient Consideration.*** This law focuses on those arrangements which purport to be a bona fide sale or exchange, but fall short of the "full consideration" measure expected between unrelated persons. If you had a $100,000 parcel of land, for example, why would you accept $35,000 for it and call it a "sale"? What you've done is made a part-sale and part-gratuitous transfer. Activities of this type — and there are many variants of them — are called transfers for "insufficient consideration."

The general rule on point is subsection (a) of Section 2043. This rule reads essentially in full as—

*If **any one** of the transfers, trusts, interests, rights, or powers enumerated and described in sections [2035, 2036, 2037, 2038, and 2041] **is made, created, exercised, or relinquished** for a* *consideration in money or money's worth, but is **not** a bona fide sale for an adequate and full consideration in money or money's worth, **there shall be included** in the gross estate only the excess of the fair market value at time of death . . . over the value of the consideration received therefor by the decedent.* [Emphasis added.]

When an item of property is required to be included "in the gross estate . . . of the decedent," it is tantamount to saying that the transfer tax shall apply. Furthermore, marital rights, which are in reality succession rights, are not treated as consideration paid [subsec. 2043(b)].

The five sections referenced in subsection 2043(a) are as follows:

Sec. 2035 — Gifts within 3 years of death,
Sec. 2036 — Transfers with retained life estate,
Sec. 2037 — Transfers taking effect at death,
Sec. 2038 — Revocable transfers, and
Sec. 2041 — Powers of appointment.

Consideration is defined solely in terms of monetary value. In other words, full and adequate consideration is the *fair market value* (FMV) as established by competent professional appraisal. Sentimental attachments, succession rights, unpaid debts, and sufficiency of consideration from a purely legal standpoint do not enter the picture. The FMV is established as if the item were offered for sale on the retail market, taking into account the nature of the item, its condition, and its usefulness to an unrelated buyer.

In 1962, the Federal Court of Appeals for the 10th Circuit (Denver, Colorado) introduced the idea that a transferor of property prior to, or upon, his death, must receive full and adequate consideration [*C. Allen, Exr.*, CA-10, 61-2 USTC ¶ 12.032; 293 F 2nd 378; cert. denied, 368 US 944]. The Court of Appeals held that a sale of property in contemplation of death of a life interest at its fair market value only reduced the value of the taxable property, rather than eliminating the cause for transfer taxation.

The Imposition Mandates

Any tax law is an "imposition" by most people's standards. The law is not a "mandate," however, until the word SHALL is expressly used or expressly implied, as in: IS HEREBY IMPOSED. The transfer tax is no exception. There are *three* transfer tax mandates.

The first is Section 2001(a): *Imposition*. It is clear, succinct, and short (25 words). It reads—

A tax is hereby imposed on the transfer of the taxable estate of every decedent who is a citizen or resident of the United States.

There is a ring of finality here: a transfer tax on "every decedent." This is why we call it the "death tax." There is no escaping the tax . . . or at least complete accountability for it. This is so whether all assets are in a living trust, or in any other kind of trust where the transfer tax has not been fully computed and paid.

The second transfer-specific mandate is Section 2501(a): *Taxable Transfers*. Its paragraph (1) reads—

A tax, computed as provided in section 2502, is hereby imposed for each calendar year, on the transfer of property by gift during such calendar year by an individual resident or nonresident. [Emphasis added.]

Note in this case that there is an annual gift tax to compute and pay. However, an annual computation is not required unless the total gifts during the taxable year exceed certain ordinary exclusion amounts. We'll present these exclusion amounts later below.

The third transfer-specific mandate is Section 2601: *Generation-Skipping Transfers*. This 16-word tax law reads—

A tax is hereby imposed on every generation-skipping transfer (within the meaning of [Generation-Skipping Transfers]*).*

The reference to "within the meaning of" includes the following tax code sections:

Sec. 2611 — Generation-skipping transfer defined.
Sec. 2612 — Taxable termination; distribution; direct skip.
Sec. 2613 — Skip person and non-skip person defined.

As you may sense on your own, the taxing of generation-skipping transfers is a complicated affair. The trustor has to determine who his skip persons are, and who his non-skips are. Even though complicated, skipping transfers can be particularly attractive to certain families. Because so, we will devote an entire chapter to this one type of trust alone. This will be our Chapter 9: Generation-Skipping Trusts. The generation-skipping tax first became effective on October 22, 1986. This GST law (as it is now called) is another one of those anti-abuse rules targeted at extended family trusts.

The "Unified" Concept

The death tax concept was first codified into tax law back in 1954. Prior to that time, many families of wealth were able to avoid most forms of general taxation. Since there was no death tax, wealth was passed down from generation to generation without there being any form of transfer tax involved. This long-standing practice (from the days of the British Kings and Lords) inevitably created social tensions and fairness problems. All of which gave birth to the idea of a transfer tax at death.

Initially, the death tax was quite modest — embarrassingly so. Nevertheless, there was some tax imposed, but it was called an excise tax (for political reasons). The low tax rates applied only after a $60,000 flat-out exclusion amount had been exceeded. Even so, very little death tax money accrued to government. This was because of the great popularity of family trusts (for those of wealth). By the time a person had reached his death bed, most wealth had been assigned irrevocably into trust. Since there was no effective gift tax then, much family money was simply "given away" in trust to successor members of the family.

It was not until 1970 that the effectiveness of a gift tax was instituted. Teeth were added by the Excise, Estate, and Gift Tax Adjustment Act of 1970. The gift tax rates then also were modest, though they were different from the death tax rates. The gift tax applied only after a one-time, lifetime exclusion of $30,000 had been claimed. This one-time exclusion was in addition to a $3,000 annual exclusion for gifts in those years.

As time went on, the confusion and overlapping of the gift and death rate structures, and the separate exclusions that were applicable, caused the transfer taxation process to be difficult to enforce. So in 1976 — via the Tax Reform Act of 1976 — Congress decided to **unify** the two separate gift tax and death tax rate structures into one. It also decided to unify the two separate exclusion amounts into one one-time life/death exclusion. This way, an individual could apply the exclusion in any manner he or she wanted. It could be applied either during life, upon death, or in some combination of the two modes. Furthermore, the annual exclusion concept for gifts retained its role, *independent* of the one-time overall exclusion amount.

The Unified Rates & Exclusions

For 20 years (1977 through 1997), the unified gift/death tax rates and the unified one-time exclusion remained the same. The basic rate structure was prescribed by Section 2001(c): *Rate Schedule*. The "schedule was one of graduated rates starting at 37% (for taxable amounts over $500,000) to 55% (for taxable amounts over $3,000,000). We present these Section 2001(c) rates to you in Figure 2.2. Briefly reviewing these graduated rates now can be very instructive. In mid-2000, there was some Congressional discussion of capping the maximum rate at 50% and readjusting the rates downward for estates under $10,000,000.

The imposition of any form of "inheritance tax" is an enigma to families of modest weatlh. They argue that they have already paid income tax. Congress is aware of this argument and may further increase the unified exclusion for estates under $3,000.000.

Section 2502(a): *Computation of* [Gift] *Tax*, refers back to the tax . . . *computed under section 2001(c)*. The effect is that which is presented in Figure 2.2. Incidentally, Section 2502(c) says—

The [gift] *tax imposed shall be paid by the donor.*

AMOUNT SUBJECT TO TENTATIVE TAX		Tax on Amount In Column A	Tax Rate on Excess Over Col. A
Amount Exceeding	But Not Exceeding	$ [Before Credits]	%
Col. A	Col. B	Col. C	Col. D
500,000	750,000	155,800	37
750,000	1,000,000	248,300	39
1,000,000	1,250,000	345,800	41
1,250,000	1,500,000	448,300	43
1,500,000	2,000,000	555,800	45
2,000,000	2,500,000	780,800	49
2,500,000	3,000,000	1,025,800	53
3,000,000	——	1,290,800	55
Above $10,000,000 a 5% surtax is added to phaseout the effect of graduated rates.			

Fig. 2.2 - The Unified Gift/Death Tax Rate Schedule

Section 2641(a): *Applicable* [GST] *Rate* references the term . . . *maximum Federal estate tax rate.* This term is defined in subsection 2641(b) as—

the maximum rate imposed by section 2001 on the estates of decedents dying at the time.

A glance at Figure 2.2 tells you that the maximum rate is 55%. In other words, a GST transfer enjoys no graduated rates whatsoever.

As to the one-time exclusion in effect in 1997, there were two separate exclusion amounts. There was a $600,000 exclusion amount for gift/death transfers. Additionally, **after** the gift/death transfer tax was computed and paid, a $1,000,000 GST exemption applied [Sec. 2631(a)].

Commencing in 1998, the $600,000 gift/death exclusion amount has been increased systematically to $1,000,000. The yearly increases are presented in Figure 2.3. Note that the $1,000,000 gift/death exclusion amount is scheduled to take effect in year 2006.

Persons Dying In -	Exclusion Amount	Equivalent Credit Against Tax
1997	$600,000	$192,800
1998	625,000	202,050
1999	650,000	211,300
2000 & 2001	675,000	220,550
2002 & 2003	700,000	229,800
2004	850,000	287,300
2005	950,000	326,300
2006 & after	1,000,000	345,800
Sec. 2010 - Unified Credit Against Estate Tax Subsec. (c) - Applicable Credit Amount		

Fig. 2.3 - Applicable Exclusion Amounts for a Transfer Estate

Using our crystal ball, the "trend lines" in Figures 2.2 and 2.3, and the GST exemption, we can see a coalescence into one overall gift/death/GST family trust exemption of $3,000,000. Of this, Trustor A (husband) gets $1,000,000; Trustor B (wife) gets $1,000,000; and the GSTs get $1,000,000. All would be inflation adjusted annually in $10,000 increments [Sec. 2631(c)].

Annual Gift Tax Exclusion

Possibly the least understood and most underused benefit of transfer taxation is the $10,000 annual gift tax exclusion. Commencing in 1998, the $10,000 is inflation adjusted annually by $1,000 increments [Sec. 2503(b)(2)].

What is misunderstood and misused is the $10,000 amount. It is not just one overall $10,000 exclusion per individual per year. The $10,000 amount is *per donor*, PER DONEE, per year. As of this writing, there is no limit to the number of donees allowed per year. There could be 5 donees (totaling $50,000); there could be 10 donees (totaling $100,000); or there could be a higher number per year. The statutory language doesn't say it quite this way, but such is the point nevertheless.

Section 2503: *Taxable Gifts*, subsection (b)(1): *Exclusions from Gifts*, puts it this way—

In the case of gifts (other than gifts of future interests in property) **made to any person** *by the donor during the calendar year, the first $10,000 of such gifts to such person for purposes of* [taxable gifts], **shall not be included in the total amount of** *gifts during such year.* [Emphasis added.]

The part about "other than gifts of future interests" means that a $10,000 amount cannot be transferred to a trust where a donee-beneficiary does not have access to it until some specified future date. The $10,000 must be gifted currently. The donee must have immediate access and use of it. A "current gift" is one by which the donor simultaneously severs all dominion and control. The donee then has total discretion on how he/she can use the $10,000. He/she can spend it, blow it, or save it.

The only exception to the prohibition of gifts of future interests pertains to transfers in trust for the benefit of a minor [subsec. 2503(c)]. The essence here is that—

No part of a gift to an individual who has not attained the age of 21 on the date of such transfer shall be considered a gift of a future interest in property.

In other words, if you start when a child reaches age 1 and make 20 annual $10,000 gifts in a custodial account for that child, by the time the child reaches age 21 there could be $200,000 (plus accrued interest, dividends, capital gains, etc.) on the line. The primary catch here is that the amount—

to the extent not so expended . . . [must] *pass to the donee on his* [her] *attaining the age 21.*

How many young adults at age 21 can manage $200,000 wisely? Not very many. And if each of **two** parents (or two grandparents) gifted $10,000 annually, the cumulative total would be $400,000 plus [$10,000/yr x 2 donors x 20 yrs]. Thus, it is imperative that every parent or grandparent raise donee children with good habits towards saving, investing, and spending money.

Taxable Gifts Cumulative

Another unique feature about the transfer taxation of gifts is that the process is cumulative. That is, all taxable gifts (those each year in excess of the annual exclusion) are aggregated continuously until death of the donor/trustor. At that time, the cumulative gift-consumed portion of the one-time unified exclusion is subtracted from the death-year amount shown in Figure 2.3. The remaining portion of the Figure 2.3 exclusion is then available for reduction of the death transfer tax.

For example, suppose at time of death the unified gift/death exclusion is $800,000. During a 10-year period of gifting before death, suppose a total of $300,000 of the one-time exclusion was consumed. That would leave a $500,000 exclusion available at time of death. To comprehend this feature properly, you must separate in your mind the various annual exclusions from the one-time unified exclusion. Each exclusion concept is independent of the other. We try to portray this important concept for you in Figure 2.4.

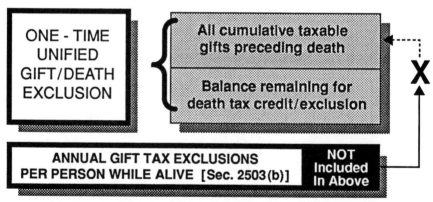

Fig. 2.4 - Independence of the Unified and Annual Exclusions

The tax law on point — Section 2502(a): *Computation of Tax* — is rather fuzzy. Nevertheless, it is instructive that we cite it for you. It reads—

The tax imposed by section 2501 [gift tax] *for each calendar year shall be an amount equal to the excess of—*

(1)   a tentative tax, computed under section 2001(c) [Fig. 2.2: unified rates], *on the aggregate sum of the taxable gifts for such calendar year and for each of the preceding calendar periods, over*

*(2)   a tentative tax, computed under such section, on **the aggregate sum of the taxable gifts for each of the preceding calendar periods**.* [Emphasis added.]

The tentative tax has a special procedural meaning of its own. It is "tentative" in the sense that it is figured on the actual taxable amount (of the aggregated taxable transfers) BEFORE the unified exclusion is applied. The "taxable amount" is the grand cumulative total of all gratuitous transfers, after applying certain deductions which are statutorily allowed. Once the taxable amount is tentatively taxed, the one-time unified exclusion is then applied. This is done in the form of an equivalent tax credit (as per the third column in Figure 2.3). The net result is a transfer tax which is enforceable by the IRS . . . and the U.S. Tax Court, if necessary.

3

GIFT & DEATH TAX RETURNS

Transferring Property Gratuitously Requires Reporting On Two Different Tax Documents. During-Life Transfers Are Valued And Taxed On Form 709; Upon Death, Transfers Are Valued And Taxed On Form 706. For Each Year That A Gift Over $10,000 Per Donee Is Made, A Form 709 Is Required. Upon Death, All Forms 709 Are Aggregated And ADDED To Form 706 For "Consumption" Of The Maximum UNIFIED Exclusion Up To $1,000,000 Per Trustor. Form 706 Is A Comprehensive INVENTORY AND APPRAISEMENT Of Each Trustor's Gross Estate, Including During-Life Transfers For Insufficient Consideration.

Now that you know a transfer tax is imposed, the next matter is: How is the tax computed and paid? Are there any special tax forms for this purpose? And if so, what are they?

In response to these questions, be advised that there are TWO basic transfer tax returns. There is a gift tax return; and, separately, there is a death tax return.

What about the generation-skipping transfer tax? Is there a separate GST tax return? No. The GST matters are folded into both the gift tax return and the death tax return. GSTs can be made during life as well as upon death.

The official titles of the two transfer tax returns are:

U.S. Gift (and Generation-Skipping Transfer) Tax Return — IRS **Form 709**

U.S. Estate (and Generation-Skipping Transfer) Tax Return
— IRS **Form 706**

Form 709 is prepared and signed by the donor of the property being gratuitously transferred. Form 706 is prepared and signed by the executor of the property being transferred from the estate of the decedent (donor/grantor/trustor). Even though there may be a trust in effect when the transfers are made, Forms 709 and 706 are not signed by the trustee, as trustee of the trust. The trustee prepares and signs an entirely separate IRS return (Form 1041), which we'll get to in a later chapter.

Not many donors/grantors/trustors are familiar with Form 709 (gifts and GSTs). Fewer still are aware of, let alone familiar with, Form 706 (deaths and GSTs). Accordingly, in this chapter we want to present the general features of Forms 709 and 706; describe the relationship between them; and indicate the respective tax computational processes. We also want to describe the supporting schedules that are required to properly complete the forms. Form 709 is an *annual* return, whereas Form 706 is a decedent's one and only final return.

Each Form 709 and Form 706 has its own bottom line: *Total transfer tax*. Each such amount is made payable to the U.S. Treasury. Once the tax is paid, the transfers of property become irrevocable . . . whether in trust or not.

Form 709 Overview

Without attachments, Form 709 (Gift and GST Tax) consists of four pages. It is accompanied by eight pages of official instructions, (about 14,000 words). The instructions on *Who Must File* say—

Only individuals are required to file gift tax returns. If a trust, estate, partnership, or corporation makes a gift, the individual beneficiaries, partners, or stockholders are considered donors. The donor is responsible for paying the gift tax. If a donor dies before filing a return, the donor's executor must file the return.

Form 709 consists of the following principal parts:

Part 1   — General Information
Part 2   — Tax Computation
Schedule A — Computation of Taxable Gifts (Including Transfers in Trust)
Schedule B — Gifts from Prior Periods
Schedule C — Computation of Generation-Skipping Transfer Tax

Schedule C is very complex. It consists of 20 columns of computations. Each column accommodates from six to ten entry amounts. As a consequence, we prefer to defer any discussion on GST matters until we get to Chapter 9: Generation-Skipping Trusts. We have many other matters to discuss before then.

There are 18 entry lines and boxes in Part 1 — General Information. Other than name, address, Tax I.D., and citizenship of the donor, there are three entries we should mention for instructional purposes. The first is—

If the donor died during the year, check here ☐ and enter date of death _____.

The second is—

Enter the total number of donees listed on Schedule A — count each person only once _____ .

The third is—

Have you (the donor) previously filed a Form 709 for any other year? ☐ Yes, ☐ No. If "Yes", has your address changed? ☐ Yes, ☐ No.

Elsewhere, the specific instructions to Part 1 say—

*A married couple may **not** file a joint gift tax return. If a gift is of community property, it is considered made one-half by each spouse. Likewise, each spouse must file a gift tax return if they have made a gift of property held by them as joint tenants or* *tenants by the entirety. However you and your spouse agree to split your gifts, you both should file your individual returns in the same envelope, to avoid correspondence from the IRS.* [Emphasis added.]

Schedules A & B: Form 709

The description of property and its value, and computational background for Form 709 derive from its Schedules A and B. Schedule A identifies the current year taxable gifts, whereas Schedule B lists all prior gift tax returns filed, and to which IRS office they were sent. Schedule A is where all the recordkeeping and foundational computations appear.

Schedule A (Form 709) consists primarily of a description of each property item, to whom it is gifted, and its fair market value. The specific columnar information required is—

Col. A — Item number
Col. B — Particulars of the gift
 • Donee's name and address
 • Relationship to donor
 • Description of gift
 • If made to a trust, enter trust's Tax I.D. and attach copy of trust instrument
 • If gift of securities, give CUSIP number (Committee on Uniform Security Identification Procedures)
Col. C — Donor's adjusted basis of gift
Col. D — Date of gift
Col. E — Value at date of gift

As to the entered valuation of a gift, a preprinted headnote to Schedule A says—

Does the value of any item listed reflect any valuation discount? ☐ *Yes,* ☐ *No. If "Yes", see instructions.*

The instructions: *Valuation Discounts*, say—

If the value of any gift you report . . . reflects a discount for lack of marketability, a minority interest, a fractional interest in real estate, blockage, market absorption, or for any other reason, answer "Yes" . . . [and] *attach an explanation giving the factual basis for the claimed discounts and the amount of discounts taken.*

We will tell you right now that valuation discounting is a prime issue with the IRS. Its initial reaction is that discountings and other undervaluations are abusive efforts to understate the amount of transfer tax. Our position is each property item that is not actual money or money equivalent should be accompanied by a professional appraisal. Human nature is such that whenever significant family wealth is being gifted away, undervaluation tends to be the rule rather than the exception.

Synopsis of 709 Computations

It is not our intention to drag you through the details of preparing Form 709. We simply want you to be aware of some of its highlights. In this regard, it is instructive to present — in abbreviated form — the computational steps as they appear on Schedule A, and the computational lines that appear on page 1. Our listing is about one-half of the total steps and lines actually shown on Form 709. You can read or skim these steps and lines as you see fit.

The bottom line of Schedule A is labeled: *Taxable gifts.* Procedurally, such amount derives as follows:

Step 1	— Total value of gifts by donor	$_____
Step 2	— Total annual exclusions for gifts listed	_____
Step 3	— Total included amount of gifts (subtract step 2 from step 1)	_____
Step 4	— Marital deduction (if any)	_____
Step 5	— Charitable deduction (if any)	_____
Step 6	— Total deduction (add steps 4 and 5)	_____

Step 7 — Subtract step 6 from step 3 _____
           Taxable gifts. Enter here and
           on line 1 on page 1 _____

The bottom line on page 1 (Tax Computation) is the current year *Transfer tax*. Procedurally, said amount derives as follows:

Line 1 — Taxable gifts from Schedule A $_____
Line 2 — Taxable prior year gifts from
          Schedule B _____
Line 3 — Total taxable gifts (*add* lines 1
          and 2) _____
Line 4 — Tax computed on line 3
          (from unified rate schedule) _____
Line 5 — Tax computed on line 2 (from
          unified rte schedule) _____
Line 6 — Tentative current-year tax
          (*subtract* line 5 from line 4) _____
Line 7 — Maximum unified credit
          against tax (exclusion equivalent) _____
Line 8 — Amount of prior periods credit
          allowable (from Schedule B) _____
Line 9 — Remaining unified credit/
          exclusion (*subtract* line 8 from
          line 7) _____
Line 10 — Current year transfer tax
          (*subtract* line 9 from line 6)
          Do not enter less than zero _____

There are other items on Form 709 that should arouse your curiosity. Perhaps it is best that you get for yourself a copy of the official form and its instructions. Particularly read the instructions titled: *Transfers Subject to Gift Tax*; *Transfers NOT Subject to Gift Tax*; *Transfers Subject to Generation-Skipping Transfer Tax*; and *Transfers Subject to an "Estate Tax Inclusion Period."* Reviewing these items on your own offers a good prelude to what to expect on Form 706 (for estates after death). In the meantime, to put Form 709 in proper perspective, we present Figure 3.1.

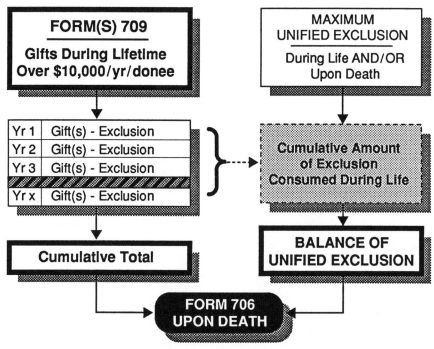

Fig. 3.1 - Cumulatively Tracking Taxable Gifts During Life

Bear in mind that for each year you make a taxable gift of more than $10,000 to any one donee, a Form 709 is required. Bear in mind also that a husband prepares his own gift tax returns, whereas a wife prepares separately her own gift tax returns. Each spouse has a taxable transfer estate of his/her own.

Form 706 Overview

Form 706: *U.S. Estate (and Generation-Skipping Transfer) Tax Return*, is a VERY FORMIDABLE document. Without attachments, it consists of 44 pages — **yes, 44 pages!** Additionally, it is accompanied by 26 pages of 3-columnar instructions: about 46,000 words! The form itself consists of five parts and 22 schedules! For introductory purposes, the five parts are—

Part 1 — Decedent and Executor
Part 2 — Tax Computation

Part 3 — Elections by the Executor
Part 4 — General Information (about 20 questions)
Part 5 — Recapitulation (of assets and deductions)

The title of Part 1: **Decedent and Executor**, makes it clear that no donor/grantor/transferor/settlor/trustor can possibly prepare his own Form 706 This is because every trustor is deceased at the time his Form 706 is required. Nevertheless, our contention is that every trustor in a family trust arrangement should have some inkling of what Form 706 is all about. To acquire this inkling, every trustor together with his intended executor should procure for himself an official copy of Form 706 and its instructions. Together they should peruse both documents and be open-eyed and realistic. We caution you that Form 706 is comprehensive.

For example, the instructions define your Gross Estate as including—

All property in which the decedent has an [ownership] *interest (including real estate outside the U.S.) . . .* [plus]

- *Certain transfers made during the decedent's life without an adequate and full consideration in money or money's worth;*
- *Annuities* [including pension plans and IRAs];
- *The includible portion of joint estates with right of survivorship;*
- *The includible portion of tenancies by the entirety;*
- *Certain life insurance proceeds;*
- *Property over which the decedent possessed a general power of appointment;*
- *Dower or curtesy (of statutory estate) of the surviving spouse;*
- *Community property to the extent of the decedent's interest as defined by applicable* [state] *law.*

No Escaping Form 706

In our opinion, a great disservice to trustors is perpetuated by many trust promoters (attorneys, financial counselors, insurance agents, and others). They convey the impression that, somehow, if a trust instrument is prepared by prestigious (and very expensive) legal talent, the need for Form 706 evaporates. The existence of Form 706 is rarely every mentioned. The prestigious talent claims to have covered all transfer-of-property "loopholes" embedded in the tax code and in unique court decisions. Our response is . . . B-A-L-O-N-E-Y.

Our challenge is this. Have your prestigious trust talent cite to you and explain IRC Section 6018: *Estate Tax Returns*. This section consists of subsection (a): *Returns by Executor*, and subsection (b): *Returns by Beneficiaries*.

If your executor, who also may be your trustee, is taken in by the prestige of the trust instrument, and overlooks preparing Form 706, subsection 6018(b) kicks in. In shorthand way, this subsection says that—

Every person holding legal or beneficial interest [in the trust property] *. . . shall . . . make a return . . . of the gross estate.*

In other words, if an executor-trustee disregards Form 706 . . . *as to any part of the gross estate of the decedent* . . . **every beneficiary** of the trust estate, individually and collectively, is responsible for Form 706. Does your trust instrument ever say this? Of course not.

Furthermore, does subsection 6018(a) say anything about a masterful trust instrument avoiding Form 706? No. But let's cite its paragraph (1) to you in full. Said paragraph reads:

Citizens or Residents — In all cases where the gross estate exceeds the applicable exclusion amount in effect under section 2010(c) [recall Figure 2.3] *for the calendar year which includes the date of death, the executor shall make a return with respect to the estate tax imposed by subtitle B* [Estate and Gift Taxes].

We see no loopholes here for trusts, do you? In fact, decedents who have trusts derive no tax advantage whatsoever over decedents who do not have trusts.

Incidentally, paragraph (2) of subsection 6018(a) addresses: *Nonresidents not citizens of the U.S..* If such a person has an estate in the U.S. of $60,000 or more, Form 706 is required. In other words, the exclusion amounts in Figure 2.3 on page 2-11 do not apply to nonresident alien decedents.

Distinction: Executor vs. Trustee

This is as good a time as any to make clear the distinction between executor functions and trustee functions. Although a trustor may name the same person (or persons) to perform both tasks, the two separate tasks cannot be performed correctly, when performed concurrently. This is another area where trust promoters are lax. They hypothesize on the ease of wearing "two hats" and combining both functions into one. This is the sure road to litigation re property valuations and premature distributions. A trustee is the distributor; an executor is the tax accountant.

An executor has total and exclusive control over inventorying a decedent's gross estate, market valuing every item of property therein, identifying all heirs and beneficiaries to such property, preparing and signing Form 706, and — of course — paying over to the U.S. Treasury the total transfer tax that has been agreed upon. It is only when this one-time gigantic task is done that the property so designated is irrevocably in trust.

The lapse of time may vary anywhere from six to 18 months normally . . . but could extend to 36 months. The completion time for Form 706 depends on the complexity of the estate, any civil litigation in process, and the extent of its scrutiny by the IRS. The executor functions are not accomplished with the snap of a finger, nor by vague wording in a trust instrument.

In Part 4 of Form 706: *General Information*, the executor is asked some 20 questions. Question 5, for example, asks for—

- *Name of individual, **trust**, or estate receiving $5,000 or more* [from the decedent's estate]
- *Identifying number* [Tax I.D.]
- *Relationship to decedent*
- *Amount (see instructions)*

The instructions at "Amount" read—

*Enter the amount actually distributed (or to be distributed) to each beneficiary **including transfers during the decedent's life**. The value to be entered need not be exact . . . [as long as] . . . the total distributions approximate the amount of gross estate **reduced by** funeral and administrative expenses, debts and mortgages, bequests to surviving spouse, charitable bequests, and any **Federal and State estate and GST taxes paid (or payable)** relating to the benefits received by the beneficiaries listed.* [Emphasis added.]

Question 12 in Part 4 above asks—

Were there in existence at the time of the decedent's death:

a. *Any trusts created by the decedent during his or her lifetime?* ☐ *Yes,* ☐ *No.*
b. *Any trusts not created by the decedent under which the decedent possessed any power, beneficial interest, or trusteeship?* ☐ *Yes,* ☐ *No.*

If you answered "Yes" to either 12a or 12b, you must attach a copy of the trust instrument for each trust.

As we try to emphasize in Figure 3.2, there are two separate tax accounting worlds out there. There is the trustor's gross estate at time of his/her death. There is the trustor's distributable trust estate which has been reduced by the amount of transfer tax paid. The executor functions in one tax world, whereas the trustee functions in a later world. The two tasks should not be intertwined.

The 9 Asset Schedules

The workhorse and backbone of Form 706 is its asset schedules. On these schedules the executor must list every item of property in which the decedent had an ownership or beneficial interest, no matter how small in value that interest may have been. Generally, each schedule has a preprinted instruction at its head, which references other schedules, tax code sections, and separate

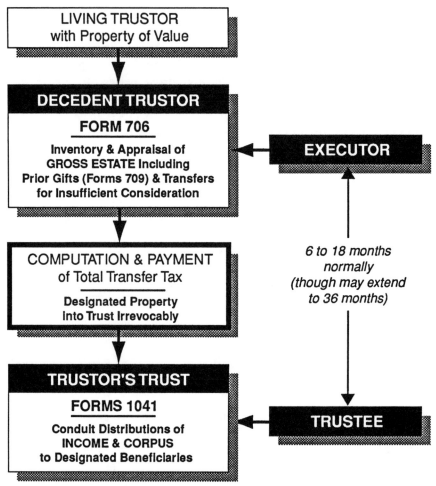

Fig. 3.2 - Distinction Between Executor Functions and Trustee Functions

instructions. There are nine of these asset schedules which we display in Figure 3.3. We also show a 10th schedule as "X". The X is a *Continuation Schedule* for any of the asset schedules. The continuation schedule appears on pages 43 and 44 of Form 706.

Most of the nine asset schedules are self-explanatory. Each requires a description of the property and its *value at date of death*. There is also a column for "alternate date," and alternate value. The alternate date may not extend more than six months after date of

Form 706	U.S. Estate Tax Return	
Part 5 - Recapitulation		
Schedule	///////////////////////////	Value at Death
///////	**Gross Estate**	///////
A	Real Estate	
B	Stocks & Bonds	
C	Mortgages, Notes, & Cash	
D	Insurance on Decedent's Life	
E	Jointly Owned Property	
F	Other Miscellaneous Property	
G	Transfers During Decedent's Life	
H	Powers of Appointment	
I	Annuities	
"X"	Continuation Schedule	as needed

Fig. 3.3 - The 9 Asset Schedules on Form 706 plus "Continuation"

death. This is to allow some options for property whose value may change significantly over short lapses of time (e.g., perishables in business, common stock, uncollectibles, etc.). The instructions point out that unless the executor *elects* alternate valuation, he/she—

> *must value all property included in the gross estate on the date of the decedent's death. Alternate valuation cannot be applied to only a part of the property. . . . You may not elect alternate valuation unless the election will **decrease** both the value of the gross estate and the total net estate and GST taxes due after application of all allowable credits.*

Most executors value at both dates, then compare the two.

One schedule that is bound to cause controversy is Schedule D: *Insurance on the Decedent's Life*. Wealthy trustors are enticed into the purchase of ILITs (Irrevocable Life Insurance Trusts). These are million-dollar-plus face value policies set up to provide liquidity for paying the taxes and debts of the estate. Insurance agents and their company attorneys insist that an ILIT is not includible in Schedule D. Yet, the IRS instructions to Schedule D put the executor in a dilemma by saying that—

> *The manner in which a policy is drawn is immaterial as long as there is an obligation, legally binding on the beneficiary, to use the proceeds to pay taxes, debts, and charges . . . for the benefit of the estate . . . even though the premiums may have been paid by a person other than the decedent.*

The whole issue of what is, and what is not, includible in the gross estate is prescribed by IRC Sections 2031 (Definition) through 2046 (Disclaimers). Particularly instructive in this regard is Section 2045: *Prior Interests*. This is the shortest of the gross estate sections (40 words). It reads in full—

> *Except as otherwise specifically provided by law, sections 2034 to 2041, inclusive, shall apply to the transfers, trusts, estates, interests, rights, powers, and relinquishment of powers, as severally enumerated and described therein, whenever made, created, arising, existing, exercised, or relinquished.* [Emphasis added.]

Section 2045 sets the mandative tone for all inclusion-noninclusion decisions re the asset schedules on Form 706. For instructive convenience, we list in Figure 3.4 the tax code sections that are pertinent to establishing a decedent's gross estate. The 17 sections lised comprise approximately 16,000 statutory words.

The Deduction Schedules

The IRS is predominantly interested in the asset schedules on Form 706. At tax rates of 50% or so, the asset schedules are the big revenue producers for the U.S. Treasury. For trustors of wealth (modest, above modest, or other), the IRS goes to great effort to scrutinize Schedules A through I.

In contrast, executors and beneficiaries are more interested in the deduction schedules. Before the death tax rates apply, the gross estate is reduced by all allowable deductions so as to arrive at a

| GROSS ESTATE OF U.S. CITIZENS OR RESIDENTS ||
IRC Sec.	Section Heading
2031	Definition of gross estate
2032	Alternate valuation
2032A	Valuation of certain farm, etc. real property
2033	Property in which decedent had an interest
2034	Dower or curtesy interests
2035	Certain gifts within 3 years of death
2036	Transfers with retained life estate
2037	Transfers taking effect at death
2038	Revocable transfers
2039	Annuities
2040	Joint interests
2041	Powers of appointment
2042	Proceeds of life insurance
2043	Transfers for insufficient consideration
2044	Previously allowed marital deduction property
2045	Prior interests
2046	Disclaimers

Fig. 3.4 - Tax Code Sections Defining a Decedent's Gross Estate

taxable estate. Obviously, the more deductions allowable, the less the taxable estate, and the less the amount of transfer tax imposed.

Altogether, there are seven deduction schedules. Each is formatted to address particular deductions, expenses, losses, and claims against the estate. The schedules (with shortened titles where appropriate) are as follows:

Sched. J — Funeral and Administrative Expenses
Sched. K — Debts, Mortgages, and Liens
Sched. L — Losses and Expenses During Administration
Sched. M — Bequests, etc. to Surviving Spouse
Sched. O — Charitable Gifts and Bequests
Sched. T — Family-Owned Business Deduction
Sched. U — Conservation Easement Exclusion

Other than Schedules K and L, we offer no particular comments. The instructions to each schedule are fairly clear. If precision is not possible, your executor is allowed to make reasonable estimates for the amounts indicated.

The full title of Schedule K is: *Debts of the Decedent, and Mortgages and Liens*. This schedule requires identifying the nature of the debt, the name of the creditor, and in columnar form the—

- Amount unpaid to date,
- Amount in contest, and
- Amount claimed as a deduction

The term "to date," can be misleading. It can mean either of two dates: date of death or date of filing Form 706. If a payment is made between date of death and date of filing, that payment is included in the amount claimed as a deduction.

The full title of Schedule L is: *Net Losses During Administration and Expenses Incurred in Administering Property not Subject to Claims*. Here, the term "Administration" is that period of time between date of death and date of the IRS's acceptance of Form 706. This is the period called: *Settlement of the decedent's estate*. If, during this period, any property is damaged or destroyed by fire, storm, theft, or other casualty, the "net loss" thereto (after any insurance reimbursement) is a deductible item.

The term "Property not subject to claims" pertains to corralling, collecting, and perfecting title to assets which are not undergoing litigation at the time Form 706 is filed. The "Expenses" are those necessary to convey title of designated property into trust, and to collect and rearrange nontrust property for direct distributions to heirs and legatees.

Other Items of Note

There are other schedules and items that we have not mentioned up to this point. They are worthy of note even though we have no intention of discussing them. They are added simply to complete our overall scoping of Form 706. We want to complete the message that Form 706 is indeed a formidable undertaking.

The particular schedules previously unmentioned are:

Sch. A-1: Section 2032A Valuation
(of certain farm and closely held business property)
Sch. P: Credit for Foreign Death Taxes
(paid to a nation having a tax treaty with the U.S.)
Sch. Q: Credit for Tax on Prior Transfers
(two decedents within 10 years of each other holding
the same property)
Sch. R: Generation-Skipping Transfer Tax
(and allocation of the GST exemption)
Sch. R-1: Generation-Skipping Transfer Tax
(for direct skips from a pre-existing trust)

Other noteworthy items referenced on Form 706 or in its instructions are:

1. Adjusted taxable gifts after 1976
(**are** includible in the tax computation part of Form 706)
2. Section 2044 property QTIP
(included in a surviving spouse's gross estate and valued on date of spouse's death)
3. GST Trust "inclusion ratio"
(where GST exemption is allocated to several skip persons; "inclusion" is non-exempt property)
4. QFOBI coordination with unified credit
(Qualified Family-Owned Business Interest deduction: Schedule T)
5. "Qualified land" for the Conservation Easement Exclusion: Schedule U

Of the above, we certainly want to cover Schedule A-1, family-owned businesses, qualified land easements, and other special valuation rules that are important to family trusts. We do so in Chapter 4: Special Valuation Rules. Surviving spouse matters, special needs family members, generation-skipping transfers, and foreign taxation will be addressed in other subsequent chapters. Meanwhile, we have to tell you how the death tax is computed.

Death Tax Computation

If you are a trustor and/or a designated executor of a deceased trustor's estate, we certainly encourage you to procure a copy of Form 706 and its instructions. Just feeling it, leafing through it, reading the general information questions, reading the schedule titles and columnar headings, and glancing at the bold-captioned wordings and acronyms (such QTIP, QDOT, QFOB) will drive home the point, we think, that no extensive trust arrangement is truly valid until all Form 706 matters are canvassed, reported, and settled . . . as determined by the IRS.

The final act in settling a trustor's estate is computing the amount of transfer tax imposed. The official sequence for doing so comprises about 60% of page 1 of Form 706. As stated earlier, this portion is captioned: **Part 2 – *Tax Computation***. There are 27 numbered lines to address. If the adjusted taxable estate exceeds $10,000,000 there are two additional lines for a 5% surtax that phases out the benefits of graduated rates for lesser estate amounts. The general sequence of events involved is block diagrammed for you in Figure 3.5.

In reviewing the computational items that back up Figure 3.5, we want to stress a few points that you might otherwise miss. Several lines down from the top (of Part 2), there is reference to all taxable gifts after 1976. These gifts (over $10,000 per year per donee) are cumulatively aggregated. These are then ADDED TO the taxable estate (gross minus deductions). A *Tentative tax No. 1* is then established (from the tax rate schedule in the instructions). The rate schedule is used **before** any credits are applied.

Between Tentative tax No. 1 and *Tentative tax No. 2*, there are adjustments for prior gift taxes paid (if any), and modification (reduction of) the one-time maximum unified credit/exclusion for any credit/exclusion consumed during the gifting years.

From Tentative tax No. 2, credits for (a) state death taxes, (b) foreign death tax, and (c) tax on prior transfers are subtracted. The result is a *Net estate tax* (before GST) as shown in Figure 3.5. By adding in the GST tax from Schedule R, the *Total transfer tax* emerges. Schedule R is a formidable schedule of its own. Its purpose is to allocate the $1,000,000 GST exemption among

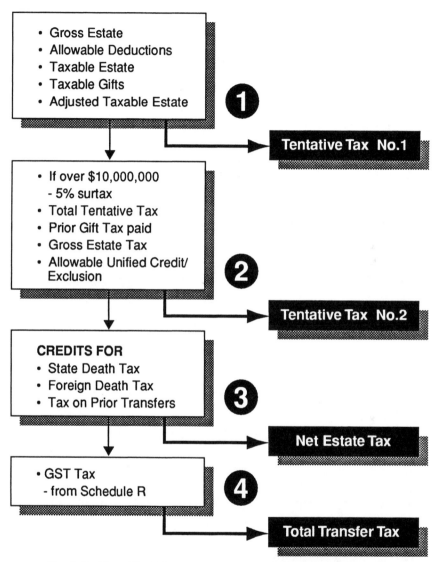

Fig. 3.5 - Simplified Diagram of Tax Computatons on Form 706

designated "skip persons." A trustor has wide latitude in the allocation process, but he must be specific. Otherwise, the IRS sets its own priorities. After said allocations, a flat 55% tax rate applies to all non-exempt property transfers.

IRS's Acceptance Letter

An estate is not settled until Form 706 is filed, all transfer tax paid, and the IRS issues its "Acceptance Letter." In general, the IRS has up to three years after the due date for filing Form 706 to review it and propose any adjustments it deems proper. In most cases, the IRS tries to accomplish this on a "fast track" . . . because much tax revenue is involved.

Every Form 706 is manually examined. In those cases where property valuations are glaringly low or heavily discounted, a detailed audit will ensue. The audit will focus primarily on real estate property valuations, life insurance proceeds and annuities, and during-life gift transfers. Keep in mind that for estates over $3,000,000 flat taxed at 55%, a few million dollars in asset undervaluations can generate significant revenue for the U.S. Treasury.

If an audit results in an IRS-proposed adjustment, the executor will receive:

STATEMENT OF ADJUSTMENT TO ACCOUNT

After paying the additional amount proposed, or as further adjusted, the IRS will then issue:

ACCEPTANCE OF ESTATE TAX RETURN

The date-of-acceptance document, stamped in the upper right-hand corner, constitutes the **date of settlement** of the deceased trustor's estate. Technically, it is the day after this date that the trust operation can begin. Recall Figure 3.2 (on page 3-12) in this regard.

Among other items listing the tentative tax, credits, and net tax, the acceptance letter states—

This letter is evidence that the Federal tax return for the estate has either been accepted as filed or has been accepted after an adjustment to which you have agreed. You should keep this letter as a permanent record. [It] will establish that your personal liability for the tax [as executor] has been settled.

4

SPECIAL VALUATION RULES

For Transfer Tax Purposes, The Term "Value" Means Fair Market Value . . . UNLESS Some Special Rule Applies. There ARE Such Rules For Family Farms, Businesses, Trusts, And Other Transfers Of Equity Interests In Property. Examples Are A $500,000 Exclusion For Conservation Easements; A $675,000 Deduction For Family-Owned Businesses; And A $750,000 Valuation Discount For Farm, Etc., Real Property. There Are Also Minority Interest Discounts (Approx. 20%) And Estate Valuation "Freezes" When Using IRS Mortality Tables. Otherwise, All Transferred Interests Which Are Not Marketable Are Disregarded.

For multi-million dollar estates, the effective transfer tax rates (after allowable deductions, etc.) are clearly in the 50% to 55% range. This fact alone raises the specter of trustors and/or their executors pursuing every scheme possible to lower the valuations on major property items. For every $1,000,000 in reduced property valuations, there is a saving of $500,000 in transfer tax. Instead of this money going to the U.S. Treasury, it would go to the beneficiaries designated by the trustor.

For certain property items, there are special rules which allow lower-than-market valuations for good cause. For example, there is Section 2031(c) which addresses: *Land Subject to a Qualified Conservation Easement*. There is also Section 2032A: *Valuation of Certain Farm, Etc. Real Property*, and Section 2057: *Family-Owned Business Interests*. Under the general gross estate inclusion rule of Section 2031, various courts have allowed limited discount factors for lack of marketability where minority ownership interests exist.

Other special valuation rules (Sections 2701–2704) take a harsher view than those above. When substantial property interests are transferred from a corporation, partnership, or trust, no discounts are allowed. This is because, usually, the transfer arrangements attempt to "build in" unrealistic undervaluations based on options, restrictions, lapsing rights, and charitable remainders.

In this chapter, therefore, we want to review and present the highlights of those valuation rules which have a major impact on Form 706 property that is designated into trust. Once in trust, Form 706 becomes the platform reference for determining income, gain, or loss during trust operations. In this regard, the term "special" means those valuations which are *other than* traditional fair market values (FMVs).

Conservation Easement Land

A trustor or his executor may "elect" to exclude from the value of certain land up to 40% of its FMV. The amount excluded, however, may not exceed $500,000 (depending on the year of death of the trustor). The special rule applicable here is Section 2031(c): *Estate Tax with Respect to Land Subject to a Qualified Conservation Easement.* This is a 2,000 word tax law with its own regulations and guidelines.

Eligible land for this special rule is that which is within 25 miles of a metropolitan area, national park, or wilderness area. Land within 10 miles of an Urban National Forest also is eligible. The land must have been owned by the trustor or a member of his family *at all times* during the 3-year period ending on the date of the trustor's death.

A "qualified conservation easement" is a restriction, granted in perpetuity, on the use that may be made of the land. Conservation purposes include: (a) its preservation for outdoor recreation or education of the public; (b) the protection of natural habitat for fish, wildlife, or plants; and (c) the preservation of open space. Land for which a charitable deduction is allowed does not qualify.

Schedule U (Form 706): *Qualified Conservation Easement Exclusion*, is used to compute the amount of exclusion from FMV. First, though, the land must be described and regularly appraised on Schedules A, B, E, F, G, and H, as appropriate. Then a 17-step computational process is followed. The computations start with the FMV of the land as reported on the gross estate schedules. Sequentially, the value of retained development rights, transfers for other charitable purposes, and the amount of indebtedness on the land are subtracted. The result is a *net value of land* to which an exclusion fraction (not to exceed 0.40) is applied. The **smaller** of this amount or the exclusion limitation of $500,000 is allowed.

Farm & Business Real Property

A very special valuation rule applies to certain farm and closely held business property. The special feature is a *special use discount* of up to $750,000 less than full market value. (The $750,000 discount is inflation-adjusted in increments of $10,000 for decedents after 1997.) The particular rule on point is Section 2032A: *Valuation of Certain Farm, Etc., Real Property*. This section comprises about 8,000 words of tax law and is accompanied by about 12,000 words of regulations This law first went into effect in 1977 after much financial pain and suffering caused by selling family farms and small businesses (real estate related) to defray the Form 706 transfer tax. In many cases, these "death tax sales" deprived deserving heirs of their customary livelihood.

To take advantage of the $750,000 valuation discount, certain conditions must be met. Among the more significant conditions are:

(1) The decedent must have been a citizen or resident of the U.S.

(2) The property must pass to a qualified heir (an ancestor, spouse, any lineal descendant of the decedent, and spouses of his lineal descendants).

(3) All heirs receiving the property must sign a tax recapture agreement, in the event the property is sold, or its qualified use abandoned, within 10 years from date of death.

(4) The property must have been devoted to a qualified farm or business use for five of the eight years prior to the decedent's death.

(5) The decedent, a member of his family, or an heir, must have "materially participated" in the management of the property and its operation.

(6) At least 50% of the adjusted gross estate must be real **and** tangible personal property devoted to the family farm and business activity.

(7) At least 25% of the adjusted gross estate must be *qualified real property.*

Qualified real property is that which is used either as a farm for farming purposes or in a trade or business other than farming. The terms "farm," "farming," and "businesses" include:

(1) stock, dairy, poultry, fruit, nut, fur-bearing animal, and truck farms;

(2) plantations, ranches, nurseries, orchards, and woodlands;

(3) structures used primarily for the raising of horticultural or agricultural commodities;

(4) the cultivation of soil, and the planting, irrigating, caring for, and harvesting the produce of land;

(5) residences and related improvements thereto occupied on a regular basis by the owners, lessees, or employees for farm maintenance and operational purposes; and

(6) roads, buildings, utilities, other structures, and improvements functionally related to farming and farm business.

Section 2032A also applies to qualifying property that passes into trust. However, such property will only be considered to the extent that a qualified heir has a present, rather than a future, interest in the trust property.

In all cases, with respect to "Section 2032A property" (as it is called), professional appraisals must be sought. Two "special use" methods are permitted, namely: (A) *Farm method* — a formula of cash rentals, real estate taxes, and effective interest rates; and (B)

Multiple factor method for closely held business — a formula of capitalizing income, fair rental values, assessed land values, and comparable sales (where nonagricultural use is not a significant factor in the sales price). Implied throughout Section 2032A is that a closely held business is one which is "closely related" to farming operations . . . where the business consists of real estate.

Must Attach Schedule A-1

Section 2032A is premised upon "special use" valuation of qualified real property. Each portion of the property that passes to a qualified heir must show both its full value and its special use value. The totals of both values are compared; the difference must not exceed $750,000. This discount amount is technically called: *Limitation on Aggregate Reduction in Fair Market Value* [subsec. 2032A(a)(2), (3)]. How is this information reported on Form 706?

This is where Schedule A-1: *Section 2032 Valuation*, comes in. Since the special use valuation applies only to real property, the Schedule A-1 must accompany Schedule A: *Real Estate*. In this regard, a headnote on Schedule A expressly states—

If you elect section 2032A valuation, you must complete Schedule A and Schedule A-1.

Schedule A-1 consists of four pages with two pages of instructions directly attached. The instructions highlight a 14-question checklist of election requirements The schedule itself is arranged in three parts, namely:

Part 1 — Type of Election
☐ Protective
☐ Regular

Part 2 — Notice of Election
☐ Farm used for farming, or
☐ Trade or business other than farming

Part 3 — Agreement to Special Valuation
   ☐ By each and every qualified heir
   ☐ Included with Form 706 when filed

Part 2 is where the valuation comparisons are made. A headnote there says—

All real property entered [in Col. A] *must also be entered on Schedules A, E, F, G, or H, as applicable.*

Part 2 consists of Columns A, B, C, and D as follows:

Col. A — Schedule and item from Form 706
Col. B — Full value (without adjustments)
Col. C — Adjusted value (for mortgages & debts)
Col. D — Value based on qualified use

The total of Column C is compared with the total of Column D. Below this comparison, specific instructions read:

[1] *Attach a legal description of all property listed* [in Col. A].
[2] *Attach copies of appraisals showing the column B values.*
[3] *Attach a description of the method used to determine the special value* [in Col. D] *based on qualified use.*
[4] *Attach affidavits describing the activities constituting material participation and the identity and relationship to the decedent of the material participants.*

A valuation discount of $750,000 translates into a transfer tax saving of about $375,000. With this magnitude of savings, if it were not for Part 3 of Schedule A-1, Section 2032A could readily blossom into widespread abuse. Part 3 is a tax repayment agreement should a qualified heir cease, or sell his portion of, the family operation. Part 3 is a legally enforceable tax document, the key words of which read:

More specifically, the undersigned heirs expressly agree and consent to personal liability under subsection (c) of 2032A [Tax

Treatment of Dispositions and Failures to Use for Qualified Use (for 10 years)] *for the additional estate and GST taxes imposed by that subsection with respect to their respective interests in the above-described property in the event of early dispositions of the property or early cessation of the qualified use of the property.*

Section 2032A is complex. We have barely scratched the surface of it. Yet, as we portray in Figure 4.1, under the right conditions, tax favorable valuations can be allowed.

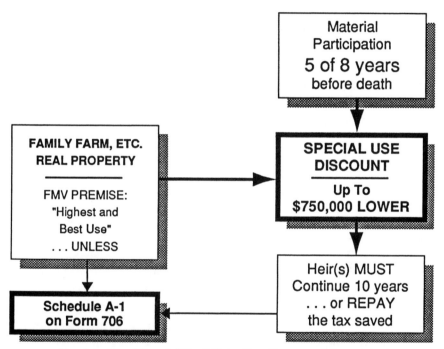

Fig. 4.1 - The "Special Use" Valuation Feature of Sec. 2032A

Family-Owned Business Interests

For nearly 20 years, Section 2032A has been the source of ambiguity over the words: "trade or business other than farming." There was always the implication that the qualifying trade or business had to relate to farming in some manner. This implication arose because more than 25% of the gross estate had to consist of "qualifying real estate." Still, many family business are passed on to qualified heirs without there being any significant real estate component. The situation has now been resolved by adding a new Section 2057 to the IR Code. Said section is applicable to the estates of trustors who died after 1997.

Section 2057 is officially titled: *Family-Owned Business Interests*. Be sure to note that the words "real property" do not appear in this title, as they do in Section 2032A. Section 2057 comprises about 4,500 tax law words, with no published regulations as yet. Except for the types of business interests that may qualify, the decedent-heir requirements of Sections 2032A and 2057 are identical. Whereas Section 2032A calls for special use valuation, Section 2057 permits a flat-out deduction against the gross estate for qualifying business interests.

A qualified family-owned business interest is an ownership interest in any trade or business, regardless of form. The ownership interests that qualify the business are—

(1)   at least 50% ownership by one family,
(2)   at least 70% ownership by two families, or
(3)   at least 90% ownership by three families.

If the business is held by more than one family, the decedent's family must own at least 30% of that business. A decedent is treated as engaged in a trade or business if any member of his family is actively engaged in the trade or business. The principal place of business (home office) must be located within the U.S.

The maximum deduction allowed by Section 2057 is $675,000. To qualify for this deduction, the aggregate value of the decedent's family-owned business interests that are passed to qualified heirs must exceed 50% of the decedent's adjusted gross estate. The "adjustments" are diminution for unpaid mortgages and indebtedness, and valid claims against the estate. The Section 2057 deduction is **in addition to** the special use valuation provisions of Section 2032A. Thus, for large estates, the $675,000 deduction provision could apply to one portion of the estate, while the $750,000 reduction-in-value provision could apply, concurrently, with another portion of the estate.

Claim on Schedule T

Under the provisions of Section 2057(e)(2): *Limitation*, passive type businesses do not qualify. The features of a passive business are such that its assets—

1. produce primarily interest, dividends, rents, royalties, and annuities;
2. are in a trust, limited partnership, or personal holding company; and
3. give rise to income from commodities trading and foreign currency exchanges.

Furthermore, a business in corporate form does not qualify if its stock and securities were publicly traded at any time within three years of the trustor's death. In short, only active, material participation, family businesses offering products and services to the public at large, on an ongoing basis, can qualify.

The allowable deduction against the value of the gross estate is computed and claimed on Schedule T (Form 706): *Qualified Family-Owned Business Interest Deduction*. This is a 4-page document consisting of—

Part 1 — Election
Part 2 — General Qualifications
Part 3 — Adjusted Value of Qualified Business
Part 4 — Qualifying Estate
Part 5 — Agreement under Section 2057

Parts 3 and 4 comprise the computational steps which, among others, require adjustments (subtractions) for mortgages, debts, claims, prior gifts, spousal transfers, and other items. The bottom line in Part 4 is the net value of the family-owned business (NOT more than $675,000) which is deductible.

In Figure 4.2 we present a brief summary of the relative roles of Schedules A-1, T, and U as they are entered in Part 5: *Recapitulation*, of Form 706. Recall that Schedule A-1 is attached to Form 706 behind Schedule A. However, its special use valuation

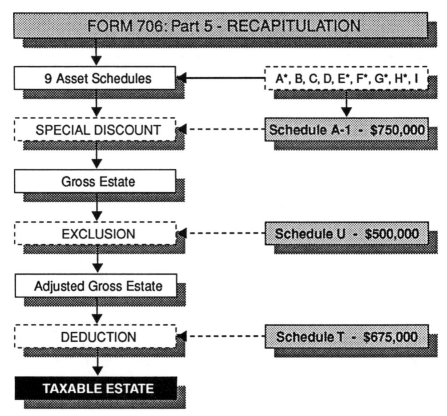

Fig. 4.2 - The Special Valuation Schedules On Form 706 Recapitulation

entries may also refer to real estate items on Schedules E, F, G, and H. We indicate this fact by an asterisk (*) in Figure 4.2. Also note that Schedule U is an *exclusion* from the gross estate, whereas Schedule T is a *deduction* against the gross estate. It's a computational "priority thing": A-1 takes precedence over U, which takes precedence over T. If the maximum allowables were attained, the overall gross estate could be reduced by as much as $1,925,000 [A-1: $750,000; U: $500,000; and T: $675,000].

Minority Interest Discounts

Section 2033: *Property in Which the Decedent Had an Interest*, reads (in full) as—

*The value of the gross estate shall include the value of all property **to the extent of the interest therein** of the decedent at the time of his death.* [Emphasis added.]

The emphasized phrase: "to the extent . . . therein," raises the issue of discounts in value for minority interests at time of death.

The general rule for establishing value is that which a willing buyer would pay to a willing seller, taking into account all facts and circumstances surrounding the marketability of the property. If a "willing seller" (in this case, the executor of a decedent trustor's estate) has a minority interest, but the majority interests are not willing sellers, what happens? For example, if a decedent had a 7% ownership interest in a $5,600,000 upscale apartment rental complex, would the includible amount in his estate be $392,000 [5,600,000 x 0.07] or some other lower amount, say, $300,000 (a 23.46% discount)?

There are no IRS regulations or guidelines on the extent of discounts that may be allowed. This is where judicial precedent comes in.

The case of *Louis F. Bonner, Sr., Est., CA-5, 96-2 USTC ¶ 60,237* sheds instructive light on the availability of fractional interest discounts. Among its many deliberations, the Bonner court noted that—

The courts have consistently . . . upheld the use of fractional interest discounts in valuing undivided interests. . . . The discount is an acknowledgment of the restrictions on the sale or transfer of property when more than one individual or entity holds undivided fractional interests. . . . Potential costs and fee associated with partition or other legal controversies among owners, along with a limited market for fractional interests and lack of control, are all considerations rationally relevant to the value of an asset.

Over the years, the judicially allowed discounts have ranged from 0% to 30%. On average a 15% discount is quite common. A 30% discount is rare; 40% is even rarer. The discounting of minority-interest property values is always a contentious issue with the IRS.

The *Estate of Alto B. Cervin, CA-5, 97-1 USTC ¶ 60,274; 111 F3d 1252* illustrates the gulf between the IRS and the executor of an estate. Alto Cervin died in 1988 at which time he owned a 50% undivided community interest in four parcels of real estate, as follows:

[1]	a 657-acre farm valued at	$650,000}	Grand Total FMV
[2]	a homestead valued at	$625,000}	$1,362,000
[3]	a parcel of land valued at	$ 27,000}	x 50%
[4]	a parcel of land valued at	$ 60,000}	= $681,000

His children owned equal shares of the other 50%. Under applicable state (Texas) law, the homestead could not be partitioned. Any partitioning of the farm and the two land parcels would involve substantial legal costs, appraisal fees, delay, and reluctance on the part of a willing buyer to assume all costs associated with a forced sale of the property. The executor thereupon claimed a 25% discount on all four parcels and entered a total of $510,750 (681,000 – 170,250) on the Schedule A of Form 706.

Upon audit of Form 706, the IRS allowed a 5% discount for parcels [1] and [2], and a 0% discount for parcels [3] and [4]. The executor disagreed, and the matter went to Tax Court in August 1992. The Tax Court sided with the IRS, whereupon the executor appealed. It was not until May 1997 — some five years later — that the Appeals Court allowed a 20% across-the-board discount for all four parcels of property.

There is an important message we are trying to convey here. While discounts for minority interests may be judicially allowed, they are not a given. If you claim more than 20%, you risk a long process of tax litigation: audits and appeals. By a "long process," we mean approximately five years!

Estate Freeze Limitation

An "estate freeze" was a strategy used by a transferor to transfer, while alive, property with a high value of retained interests that literally evaporated at time of death. A gift tax return (Form 709) was filed which fixed — *froze* — the property value at time of gift rather than at time of death. This strategy was mostly used by donors/trustors/transferors with large holdings in real estate, and by highly successful family businesses. The idea was to shift all built-in capital gains from a senior member of a family to one or more junior members.

To illustrate the freeze strategy, consider a senior member who held a $3,000,000 equity interest in a family business corporation. He transferred 100 *nonvoting* shares to a junior member with an equity interest of $1,000,000. The senior member retained 200 voting shares with an equity interest of $2,000,000. The transfer arrangement called for the voting power of the 200 shares to lapse (vanish) upon death of the transferor. At such time, the 100 nonvoting shares automatically converted to their full voting power. In the meantime, the $3,000,000 property interests appreciated to $5,000,000. The net effect is that the freeze strategy saved the deceased trustor's estate $4,000,000. The transfer tax saving was $2,000,000 (approximately). Naturally, the higher the amount of family wealth at stake, the more aggressive were estate freeze strategies pursued.

In 1987, Congress sought to remedy the abuses of estate freezing by enacting Section 2036(c): *Inclusion Related to Valuation Freezes.* This law didn't work very well. So, in 1990, congress repealed Section 2036(c) and replaced it with *four* entirely new retained interest laws. The four laws, all effective for gift-type transfers after October 8, 1990 are:

Sec. 2701 — Special Valuation Rules in Case of Transfers of Certain Interests in Corporations or Partnerships.
Sec. 2702 — Special Valuation Rules in Case of Transfers of Interests in Trusts.
Sec. 2703 — Certain Rights and Restrictions Disregarded.
Sec. 2704 — Treatment of Certain Lapsing Rights and Restrictions.

We summarize the high points of these laws in Figure 4.3. Consisting of a grand total of about 5,000 tax law words, we cannot

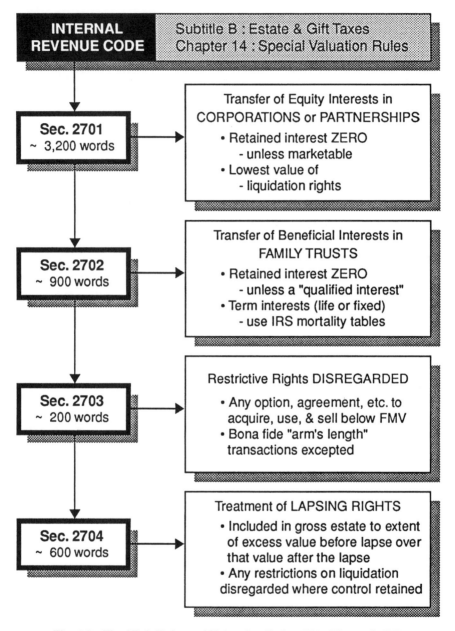

Fig. 4.3 - The High Points of Valuation Rules 2701 Through 2704

possibly cover them all. The objective of these new sections is to reduce the abuses in estate freeze valuations. This is sought to be accomplished by addressing the marketability issue of retained interests. If the retained interests by senior family members have no marketable value to the general public, or are not the result of a bona fide business transaction with a nonfamily person or entity, they are disregarded altogether. This is the substance of Section 2703 above. This is also the long-held position of the IRS. Either prove the market value of an item by independent means, or its value is zero.

Sections 2701 & 2702: Synopsis

Of the four valuation rules listed above, Section 2701 is by far the most complex. It is directed at corporations and partnerships where one or more family members control 50% or more of the equity interests of the entity. The essence is that any retained right, except a distribution right, is valued at zero. This maximizes the value of the transferred interest for tax purposes. If a distribution right is accompanied by a qualified payment (in money or money's worth), only the **lowest valuation** of said right is recognized. Again, this maximizes the value of the transferred interest.

As per subsection (b)(2): *Control,* the term means—

(A) *Corporations — the holding of at least 50% (by vote or value) of the stock of the corporation.*

(B) *Partnerships — (i) the holding of at least 50% of the capital or profit interests in the partnership, or (ii) the holding of any interest as a general partner . . . in a limited partnership.*

As per subsection (a)(2): *Exceptions for Marketable Retained Interests,* the zero or lowest value rule . . .

shall not apply to any right retained . . . if—

(A) *market quotations are readily available . . . for the retained interest,*

> (B) *the retained interest is the same class as the transferred interest, or*
>
> (C) *the retained interest is proportionally the same as the transferred interest, without regard to nonlapsing difference in voting power . . . or management control.*

The treatment of lapsing rights, liquidation rights, and transfer restrictions in a corporation or partnership is addressed by Section 2704. The tax treatment (in contrast to state law treatment) rests entirely upon the differences (if any) in extent of control before and after the transfer of an equity. If there is no discernible change in control, any estate freeze value is zero. If there is a determinable FMV difference in before and after control, the lowest value of that difference becomes its freeze value. The FMV of the untransferred control is included in the transferor's gross estate upon his death.

Section 2702 is directed at the transfers of interests in trusts to a "member of the family" or to an "applicable family member." Unless an exception applies, the retained interest is valued pursuant to subsection 2702(a)(2): *Valuation of Retained Interests*. The statutory language is clear. It reads—

> (A) *In general — The value of any retained interest which is not a qualified interest **shall be treated as being zero**.*
>
> (B) *Valuation of qualified interest — The value of any retained interest which is a qualified interest shall be determined under* [IRS Valuation Tables].

Subsection (c)(4)(B): *Valuation Rule for Certain Term Interests*, goes on to say—

> *The value of such term interest . . . shall be the amount which the holder of the term interest establishes as the amount for which such interest could be sold to an unrelated third party.*

How do you value a family interest in property where no offer is intended to be made to an unrelated third party?

5

GRANTOR TRUST RULES

Special Rules Have Been Enacted [IRC Sections 671-679] To Tax Test The Validity Of Trusts. These Rules Focus On Those Powers Which Deprive The Beneficiaries Of Their Full Beneficial Rights To The Trust Property. Deprivation Results From Reversionary Interests, Diversion Of Income, Assignment Of Corpus, Adverse Influences, And Self-Dealings By Grantors (And Nongrantors). When These "Powers" Reach More Than 5% Of The Trust Property Value, The Grantor Is Treated As SUBSTANTIAL OWNER Of That Trust. He Is Then Taxed On Its Income, And Its Corpus Reverts To His Gross Estate.

For many years, Congress has been concerned about the misuse of family trusts by those of wealth. So much so that on March 1, 1986 it enacted a new body of tax law directed at "Grantor Trusts." The more formal titled assigned is: *Grantors and Others Treated as Substantial Owners*. This body of law, Sections 671 through 679, is codified as Supbart E of Subchapter J: *Estates, Trusts, Beneficiaries, and Decedents* . . . of the Internal Revenue Code.

In pure legal terms, a "grantor" is one who conveys property or property interests to another person or entity, either formally or informally, either for consideration (money's worth) or without consideration. In whatever manner the conveyance is made, a grantor relies on the legalese and ambiguity surrounding contractual arrangements to avoid the transfer tax discussed in Chapter 2. Yet, the terms "grantor" and "trustor" functionally are one and the same. He/she who creates a trust and transfers property to it is a grantor or trustor depending on the ends served.

A grantor trust is a questionable trust. It is a trust in form but not in substance. The creator generally wants it both ways. He wants the legal formality of a trust yet he doesn't want to give up all dominion and control over the property he has conveyed — or intends to convey — to the trust. He wants to keep his fingers on a few strings that he can pull at any time.

This is where the grantor trust tax rules come into play. The rules try to detect what the strings are, and who can tug on them. He who can tug on the strings — whether he actually does so or not — is treated as the "substantial owner" of that portion of the trust property. The reality is that the trust property may not be owned by the trust for the exclusive benefit of the beneficiaries as would be the case of a bona fide family trust.

The purpose of the tax rules on grantor trusts is to question who has substantive power over the trust property. What the trust instrument says is not always relevant. What is important is "substance over form." When you create a trust irrevocably, there must be genuine economic substance to, and absolute severance of control over, the property conveyances thereto.

There are 10 grantor trust rules that you need to know about. We'll address all 10 in this chapter. After our presenting them to you, we want you to think of them as anti-abuse rules for keeping you (and your trust) on the straight and narrow. Once you start thinking this way, you'll sense why grantor trusts — often cited as: *abusive family trusts* — are seldom accepted as prima facie fact. If the trust instrument that has been prepared for you looks and sounds too good to be true, insist that your preparer "test the trust" under the rules below.

Rule 1: Substantial Owner: $5^{+}\%$

Ordinarily, the designated beneficiaries are the ultimate owners of trust property. This means that once property is in a tax qualified trust, the beneficiaries collectively have 100% *distributive rights* to that property. If there are four beneficiaries, for example, each may co-own equally 25% of those rights, or they could co-own unequally any portion from 5% on up per beneficiary. In the context of ownership control, a portion less than 5% is generally considered to be de minimis or negligible.

In the sequence of events that establishes the trust property, if any person or entity exercises — or can exercise — *any form of control* over that property for his or her or its benefit, such person or entity may be deemed the "substantial owner" thereof. The substantial ownership rule applies to each "attributable portion" of the trust property, rather than to the entire trust itself. This means that there can be more than one substantial owner at a given time, whereby each owns a (different) separate portion.

In years prior to 1986, the term "substantial owner" was never quantified. This was because the disputive issues between grantors/trustors and the IRS focused on the term *incidents of ownership* as being determinative of power and control.

Effective March 1, 1986, Congress set a specific quantitative value as to what constitutes substantial ownership. It prescribed that if there were a *more than 5% possibility* of anyone interrupting or interfering with the distributive rights of the beneficiaries, said person or entity became a substantial owner. The inference was that each said more-than-5% owner's portion of the trust property would have to be separately determined. Each owner's allocable portion would be further separated into an income portion and a principal (or corpus) portion. When so, each substantial owner is taxed prorata on his portion of the income, and correspondingly, his prorata portion of the corpus reverts to his gross estate.

We present in Figure 5.1 a simplified version of the substantial owner concept. Rule 1 applies only to that portion of the trust where the exercise of any power will diminish the full beneficial enjoyment of that property by the beneficiaries. After all, the purpose of a gratuitous trust is to convey property to it . . . irrevocably.

To determine if someone other than the designated beneficiaries is a substantial owner of *any portion* of the trust property, various "tests" are applied. These tests are the focus of Rules 2 through 10 which follow. As we'll see in these rules, a substantial owner can be anyone — grantor or nongrantor — who is associated directly or indirectly with the administration of the trust.

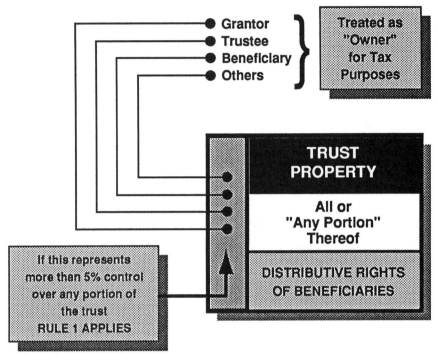

Fig. 5.1 - Owners With "Strings Attached" to Trust Property

Rule 2: Reversionary Interests

If a grantor sets up a trust with no strings attached to the property he has conveyed to it, it is said that he has no reversionary interests in that property. He has severed all dominion and control over it. Complete severance of property interests does not sit will with many family trust grantors. The universal desire, it seems, is to retain some reversionary power over the property. Grantors seek to do this as inconspicuously as possible.

In everyday terms, a "reversionary interest" exists when—

(1) there is reversion of any portion of the trust property to the grantor after creation of the trust;

(2) there is reservation of some power by the grantor to determine who should enjoy the corpus or income; or

(3)   there is reservation of some important administrative control which the grantor exercises in a nontrustee capacity.

When any of these circumstances exists, the grantor is treated as the substantial owner of that portion of the trust property to which the reversionary interest applies. He is taxed accordingly.

The general rule on reversionary interests is stated forcefully in Section 673(a) of the IR Code. This subsection reads in full as—

*The grantor **shall be treated** as the owner of any portion of a trust in which he has a reversionary interest in either the corpus or the income therefrom, if, as of the **inception** of that portion of the trust the value of such interest **exceeds 5 percent** of the value of such portion.* [Emphasis added.]

Then, subsection 673(c) goes on to say—

For purposes of subsection (a), the value of the grantor's reversionary interest shall be determined by assuming the maximum exercise of discretion in favor of the grantor.

In other words, **each time** there is an "inception" of property (conveyance) into the trust, that portion granted has to be then valued. Next, the nature and extent of any retained power that attaches to that property, if any, has to be established. The tax presumption is that the retained power (reversionary interest) will be used to the maximum benefit of the grantor. The consequence is that the *maximum benefit* to the grantor becomes the standard for determining whether the 5% threshold has been exceeded. Whether the grantor actually exercises his reversionary power or not is irrelevant. The fact that he has retained any power at all over the property assumes that, given the opportunity or need, it will be used.

Rule 3: Grantor's Spouse, Etc.

A grantor cannot circumvent Rule 2 by letting his spouse assume the reversionary interests. This opportunity is blocked totally by IRC Section 672(e): ***Grantor Treated as Holding Any Power or Interest of Grantor's Spouse***. This subsection reads in key part as—

(1)   A grantor shall be treated as holding any power or interest held by—
(A) any individual who was the spouse of the grantor at the time of the creation of such power or interest, or
(B) any individual who became the spouse of the grantor after the creation of such power or interest.

(2)   An individual legally separated from his spouse under a decree of divorce or of separate maintenance shall not be considered as married.

The obvious reason for paragraph (2) above is not to invalidate alimony trusts. Said trusts are "qualified" if they are incident to divorce, and the grantor settles his marital obligation in one lump sum by funding a separate trust for his ex-spouse.

In addition to the spousal inclusion in Rule 2 (when the spouses are living together), there are other grantor inclusions. A grantor will be treated as the owner of a trust by virtue of certain powers exercisable by trustees. This is particularly true of the grantor's spouse is a trustee or if more than half of the trustees are related or subordinate parties, subservient to the wishes of the grantor or his spouse. Related or subordinate parties are—

The grantor's [or grantor's spouse's] *father, mother, issue, brother or sister, an employee of the grantor; a corporation or any employee of a corporation in which the stock holdings of the grantor and the trust are significant from the viewpoint of voting control; a subordinate employee of a corporation in which the grantor is an executive* [Sec. 672(c)(2)].

No matter which way a grantor turns in his circle of relatives, friends, and business associates, if any of them act as trustees for his trust, tax avoidance suspicion can be aroused. Even more so, should the trust make unsecured loans to the grantor or his spouse.

These suspicions, however, can be refuted by the grantor's showing — very convincingly — that his designated trustees are acting solely and purely as trustees, and are not under any influence from him whatsoever. If the grantor really and truly has severed his dominion and control over the trust property, a showing of nonreversionary interest is not difficult.

Rule 4: Death of Beneficiaries

There are two modifications to the reversionary interest rule. They key modification is an exception to the rule where a minor lineal descendant of the grantor dies before attaining age 21. The grantor is not treated as the owner of such trust during the minor beneficiary's life, even if the minor's portion of the trust property reverts fully to the grantor after the minor's death.

The statutory wording on point is tax code Section 673(b): *Reversionary Interest Taking Effect at Death of Minor Lineal Descendant Beneficiary*. This statute reads in essential part as—

In the case of any beneficiary who—

(1) is a lineal descendant of the grantor, and

*(2) holds all of the present interests in any portion of a trust, the grantor **shall not** be treated . . . as the owner of such portion, solely by reason of a reversionary interest in such portion which takes effect upon the death of such beneficiary, before such beneficiary attains age 21.* [Emphasis added.]

The second modification is a postponement of the reversionary interest rule, rather than an outright exception to it. This postponement of a reacquired interest is addressed in Section 673(d): *Postponement of Date Specified for Reacquisition*. This section treats the grantor's reacquisition of a property interest after the death of an adult beneficiary as a "new start" for that portion of the trust property. The focal statutory phrase is: *. . . shall be treated as a new transfer in trust commencing on the date on which the postponement is effective.* This modification applies only if all income attributable to the adult deceased beneficiary (regardless of his life expectancy) was indeed taxed to the beneficiary during that beneficiary's life.

Otherwise, the reversionary interest rule (Rules 2 and 3, actually) soundly repeals prior law recognizing so-called: 10-year trusts. Prior to 1986, reversionary interests to the grantor were fully allowed, provided they took place after 10 years from the date the property was transferred into trust.

Rule 5: Beneficial Enjoyment

Ordinarily, the designated beneficiaries are entitled fully to the distributions and enjoyment of trust property, in accordance with the terms of the trust instrument. If any "shifting" of this beneficial enjoyment can be done without the consent of the beneficiaries themselves, the grantor becomes the owner of the distributions. He is then taxed accordingly. This is the thrust of Rule 5 [Sec. 674]: *Power to Control Beneficial Enjoyment.*

Subsection 674(a): *General Rule*, reads in full as follows:

The grantor shall be treated as the owner of any portion of a trust in respect of which the beneficial enjoyment of the corpus or the income therefrom is subject to a power of disposition, exercisable by the grantor or a nonadverse party, or both, without the approval or consent of any adverse party.

The above use of the terms "nonadverse party" and "adverse party" may be a little confusing. If you read the word "nonadverse" as being a nonbeneficiary, and the word "adverse" as being a beneficiary, the meanings become more direct. In all cases, the term "party" applies to any person or entity who participates, directly or indirectly, in the administration of the trust.

The power to shift beneficial enjoyment among the beneficiaries consists of the following type activities:

1. The arbitrary allocation of receipts and disbursements between income and corpus.
2. "Slanting" the distributions to primarily favor one beneficiary at the expense of the others.

3. Unexplained off-and-on decisions to distribute or not distribute the income.
4. The power to "sprinkle" the income or corpus among the current beneficiaries.
5. The power to shift income or corpus from current beneficiaries to remaindermen (those receiving benefits upon termination of the trust).

There are a number of statutory exceptions to Rule 5. In fact, there are 10 such exceptions. They are addressed in tax code subsections 674(b) through 674(d). We summarize these for you in Figure 5.2.

GRANTOR RULE 5	POWER TO CONTROL BENEFICIAL ENJOYMENT
Exception IRC Sec. No.	Description
674 (b) (1)	Income applied to support of dependent
674 (b) (2)	Enjoyment affected only after specific event
674 (b) (3)	When excercisable only by decedent's will
674 (b) (4)	When allocable among designated charities
674 (b) (5)	Distribution of corpus based on "definite standard"
674 (b) (6)	Income withheld temporarily, then paid
674 (b) (7)	Income withheld during disability of payee
674 (b) (8)	Accountable allocations between income and corpus
674 (c)	income/corpus apportionments by independent trustee
674 (d)	Income allocations on "reasonably definite standard"

Fig. 5.2 - Statutory Exceptions to Rule 5 [IRC Sec. 674]

Basically, the exceptions in Figure 5.2 are those which you'd expect to find in any well prepared trust instrument, with an independent trustee. The whole idea of a proper trust is to set the terms of the distributions to beneficiaries, then leave the trustee alone to do his job. Any *influence tugging* at the trustee by the grantor or other nonbeneficiary defeats the professed trust purpose.

Rule 6: Administrative Control

Often in the past, reciprocal trusts have been set up between close family members — typically, husband and wife — where each grantor becomes the trustee/beneficiary of the other's trust. They establish virtually identical trusts, with broad administrative powers being granted to each trustee. The effect is as though each grantor had created, in favor of himself, a trust that is now invalid under the above-cited rules. Rule 6, therefore, is a reconfirmation of the no-benefit-to-grantor concept where broad administrative powers can be exercised. If such powers are too broad, and they are exercisable for the benefit of the grantor, they are tantamount to administrative control of the trust by the grantor. After all, the whole idea of a family trust is to preserve the assets for distribution, ultimately, to designated beneficiaries.

Administrative control for the benefit of the grantor is the test for taxing him. Regardless of the duration of the trust, its income is taxable to the grantor where, under circumstances attendant upon its operation, administrative control is exercisable primarily for the benefit of the grantor or the grantor's spouse rather than for the beneficiaries of the trust.

This test for taxing the grantor is statutorily expressed in Code Section 675 as—

The grantor shall be treated as the owner of any portion of a trust in respect of which [there is] *a power exercisable by the grantor or a nonadverse part to—*

(1) purchase, exchange, dispose of, or otherwise deal with [trust property] *for less than adequate consideration in money or money's worth.*

(2) borrow the corpus or income, directly or indirectly, without adequate interest or without adequate security.

(3) [reborrow] *with adequate interest and security those trust funds which have not been completely repaid . . . before the beginning of the taxable year.*

(4) direct the voting of stock or other securities of a corporation in which the holdings of the grantor and the trust are significant from the viewpoint of voting control, or

(5) reacquire the trust corpus by substituting other property of equivalent value.

The idea behind this rule (Rule 6: Sec. 675) is to prohibit those administrative actions which give the grantor an economic benefit from the trust. To the extent that the grantor benefits, he deprives the beneficiaries of those same benefits. Again, this sort of dealing defeats the professed purpose of a trust.

Rule 7: Income for Grantor

Under the assignment-of-income doctrine, one cannot arbitrarily divest the ownership of income from the ownership of the underlying property from which the income derives. And so it is with trust income. Ordinarily, such income belongs to the beneficiaries because they are the distributee owners of the trust property. That is, provided that the grantor or other nonbeneficiary has severed all interests in the trust property. Nevertheless, as is always the case, the grantor can carve out for himself a portion of the property from which the income accrues to him alone. As to the specified portion, the grantor is the owner of that portion as well as the income from it. Said income usually can be ascertained readily from the nature and use of the property.

There are bona fide situations where there are discretionary powers to distribute, accumulate, or pay to someone other than the grantor for the grantor's benefit, the trust income. In these cases, the grantor automatically becomes the owner of that portion of the trust property, whether he intends this or not. Whoever generates and receives income is the owner of that income. This is the essence of Grantor Rule 7 (Sec. 677): *Income for Benefit of Grantor.*

Subsection 677(a) specifies that—

The grantor shall be treated as owner of any portion of a trust, . . . whose income without the approval or consent of any [beneficiary] *is, or, in the discretion of the grantor or a* [nonbeneficiary], *or both, may be—*

(1)   distributed to the grantor or the grantor's spouse,
(2)   held or accumulated for future distribution to the grantor or the grantor's spouse, or
(3)   applied to the payment of premiums on policies of insurance on the life of the grantor or the grantor's spouse.

The idea here is that any discretionary assignment of trust income to the grantor deprives the beneficiaries of their full beneficial enjoyment of the trust property.   However, if *any* beneficiary approves or consents to the assignment, the trust is treated as being owned by the trustee for the beneficiaries: not by the grantor.

Similarly, the grantor is not the owner in those situations where his income assignment commences after the occurrence of some specific event, or upon a legal obligation imposed on him to support and maintain a beneficiary (other than his spouse and minor children).

Rule 8: Nongrantor Owners

In closely-held family trusts, a trustee, beneficiary, or some other nongrantor third party may be treated as the owner of the trust, rather than the grantor. These situations arise when the nongrantor acquires sufficient power, exercisable by himself, to vest corpus or income in himself or his spouse.   This can happen when a beneficiary is also a trustee or co-trustee. The net result is that he who has the power to receive income upon demand, or the power to terminate the trust and receive its corpus, is treated s the owner. This is the underlying concept of the term: *power of appointment* (of property interests). The mere possession of this power indicates ownership, whether the power is exercised or not.

Such is the substance of Rule 8 [Sec. 678]: *Person other than Grantor Treated as Substantial Owner*.   The general rule is subsection 678(a), which reads in part—

A person other than the grantor shall be treated as the owner of any portion of a trust with respect to which:

(1)   such person has a power exercisable solely by himself to vest the corpus or the income therefrom in himself, or

(2)   such person has previously partially released or otherwise modified such a power and after the release or modification retains such control as would . . . subject a grantor of a trust as the owner thereof.

There are two exceptions to this nongrantor owner rule. One exception is where the grantor — as originally granted or thereafter modified — is already treated as the owner. The rationale here is that there cannot be two owners of the same trust property at the same time [Sec. 678(b)].

The second exception is where the deemed nongrantor owner renounces or disclaims his ownership control [Sec. 678(d)]. He must do this in writing and within a reasonable period of time after becoming aware of his powers. Usually, this awareness follows on the advice of some trust professional who is concerned that the trust purpose, perhaps unintentionally, is being violated.

Rule 9:   Foreign Transfers

Transfers of property by U.S. persons into foreign trusts is one of the most watched-over activities of federal tax administration. The rules on foreign trusts were first enacted in 1976, and are becoming more rigorously enforced every passing year. The pure essence of these rules is that if, **anywhere** in the chain of transactional and administrative events, there is a U.S. beneficiary involved, or a U.S. person who can be treated as a beneficiary, that person or beneficiary is the owner of the trust. All of those clever schemes of control via foreign corporations, foreign partnerships, and foreign trustees are for naught. Foreign trusts are not illegal; it is just that you have to disclose the extent of your interests therein.

Tax code subsection 679(c) makes the above quite clear. This subsection reads in part as—

A [foreign] trust shall be treated as having a U.S. beneficiary for the taxable year unless—

(A) under the terms of the trust, no part of the income or corpus of the trust may be paid or accumulated during the taxable year to or for the benefit of a U.S. person, and

(B) if the trust were terminated . . . no part of the income or corpus of such trust could be paid to or for the benefit of a U.S. person. [Emphasis added.]

For purposes of this rule, a "U.S. person" is defined as having more than 50% voting rights in a foreign corporation; having an interest in a foreign partnership; or having any influence over a foreign trustee. Thus, except for paragraphs (A) and (B) above, transfers by reason of death, and transfers where all the gain is fully taxable in the U.S., there is no way around Grantor Rule 9 [Sec. 679]: ***Foreign Trusts Having One or More U.S. Beneficiaries.***

Rule 9 says very emphatically that—

*A U.S. person who **directly or indirectly** transfers property to foreign trust . . . shall be treated as the owner for his taxable year of **the portion** of such trust **attributable to** such property, if for such year, there is a U.S. beneficiary of **any portion** of such trust.* [Emphasis added.]

These emphasized phrases are to point out that foreign trusts are questioned on a year-by-year basis. That is, if, in any year, there is ANY PORTION attributable to a U.S. person, that or other U.S. person becomes the owner thereof. The implication is that "attributable" U.S. persons can come and go. The only way to detect this is to screen annually every foreign trust operation. The screening is done on Schedule B of your yearly Form 1040, at Part III. This is the part that asks you questions about foreign accounts and foreign trusts. Do you have such accounts? ☐ Yes, ☐ No. Did you create or transfer to a foreign trust? ☐ Yes, ☐ No. If you answer "Yes" to either question, you must file additional information forms.

Rule 10: Power to Revoke

To revoke means: *to withdraw, repeal, rescind, cancel, or annul.* As such, it should be self-evident that he who has the power to revoke a trust, or any portion of it, is the owner thereof. This is true whether the person is a grantor or nongrantor. The end result of revocation is as though the trust were never created in the first place. The power to revoke is a far superior power to any reversionary interest (Rule 2) that a creator may have.

Rule 10 [Sec. 676]: *Power to Revoke*, therefore, says—

The grantor shall be treated as the owner of any portion of a trust, whether or not he is treated as such owner under any other [grantor rule] *. . . where **at any time** the power to revest in the grantor title to such portion is exercisable by the grantor or a nonadverse party, or both.* [Emphasis added.]

Although not expressly an exception, there is only one modification to Rule 10. If, under the terms of the trust instrument, the grantor/nongrantor cannot possibly revoke the trust until after the occurrence of some specified event (such as the death of the principal beneficiary), he will not be treated as the owner during that period of time [Sec. 676(b)]. This condition usually involves some form of reversionary interest, subsequent to the event, which the grantor may exercise or relinquish. If he does not relinquish his reversionary interest, said interest is treated as the power to revoke.

We can restate Rule 10 in another way. If title to a portion of the trust will revest in the grantor upon the exercise of a power, the grantor will be treated as the owner of that portion, regardless of whether the power is to revoke, to terminate, to alter or amend, or to appoint. A power to revest or revoke is the economic equivalent to a reversion.

A grantor's power to revoke is the thesis on which the euphorically popular "living trusts" are premised. They are revocable at any time while the grantor is alive. This means that said trusts are really nontrusts until after the grantor deceases. At that time, the property in the trust and that designated for it become irrevocable. That is, after all transfer taxes are computed and paid.

Effect of Being "Owner"

Throughout all of the Grantor Rules 1 through 10, there is one consistent phrase. The phrase is—

*. . . shall be treated as the **owner** of . . .*

This should raise a question in your mind. Why is it so important that a grantor be treated as the owner of a trust?

There are two reasons, actually.

One, the grantor pays tax on the income generated by that portion of the trust which is attributable to his ownership powers. He can't conduit it through to the beneficiaries. After he pays tax on the income, he can give it to the beneficiaries as a personal gift. The effect is no different from not having a trust in the first place. Anyone — grantor or nongrantor — can give away as much as $10,000 per year PER DONEE, without tax consequences.

The second and by far the more important reason has to do with death tax: more properly, transfer tax.

Most often, trusts are set up during the life of a grantor to get as much growth-type property as possible in, before the grantor dies. Property which is properly in trust, where the grantor is not treated as the owner thereof, remains outside of his estate for death tax purposes. For a grantor whose assets may well exceed $3,000,000, property in trust before death becomes a powerful tax incentive. With death tax rates in the 35% to 55% range, a few million dollars in trust before death can save big bucks.

It is because of the death tax that the grantor rules have been made intentionally harsh. The thrust behind these rules is to quash all trust forms where the primary motivation is for tax reasons rather than for pure trust reasons. A trust is NOT a tax shelter.

Fortunately, there is a beneficial side to the grantor trust rules. They are intended to protect the interests of the beneficiaries once the property — or a portion of it — is irrevocably in trust. The underlying idea of a family trust is to **preserve** the property therein, use it for generating income, then ultimately pass it on to the beneficiaries at the time of their need.

6

CHARITABLE REMAINDER TRUSTS

The Only Trust Form That Provides Significant Tax Deductions (Income, Gift, Death) To A Trustor Is A Charitable Remainder. At Least 10% Of The Trust Assets Must Be So Designatad. The Remainder FRACTION Is Determined From IRS ACTUARIAL TABLES Based On The Latest Census Of U.S. Mortality. When More Than 2 Persons Are Designated As Living Recipients, A Distinction Between "Life Interests" And Nonlife Interests Is Required. Fixed Distributions To Noncharitable Beneficiaries Are MANDATORY, Whereas The Timing Of Contributions To Charity Is Discretionary.

For above-modest wealth estates, charitable remainder trusts (CRTs) play a major role in family estate planning. A chunk of the wealth — certainly not all of it — can be dedicated to a CRT for the benefit of a trustor and his spouse while alive. After the surviving spouse dies, the remainder in the trust (both income and corpus) goes to a qualified charity. Because the qualifying charity is tax exempt, the CRT itself is tax exempt. During the pre-remainder drawdown period, however, there are tax consequences to, and tax returns to be filed by, the noncharitable recipient(s).

There is a certain "tax beauty" to a CRT. It derives from official valuation tables that the IRS publishes. (Recall our discussion in the latter part of Chapter 4.) Using the IRS's own actuarial and interest rate tables, a trust preparer can predetermine the *present value* of a charitable remainder . . . some one or two lives down the road.

Once the present value is known, the trustor has the choice of using the charitable remainder either as an income tax deduction, a gift tax deduction, or a death tax deduction. For persons in the maximum tax brackets, charitable deductions become a powerful motivation.

Because of charitable deduction benefits, abuses have crept into CRT arrangements over the years. The abuses include: (a) overvaluation of the charitable remainder amount; (b) directing the remainder to a private foundation in which family members can exercise influence; and (c) fee milking by administrative agents (including family members) for the trust entity. As a consequence of these and other abuses, Congress has tightened up on the CRT rules for property transfers after July 28, 1997.

Accordingly, in this chapter we want to review with you the CRT rules as they appear in the Internal Revenue Code and its regulations. We also want to describe the features of a charitable remainder ANNUITY trust (CRAT) and a charitable remainder UNITRUST (CRUT), and explain why such entities are so highly acceptable to the IRS. Additionally, we want to give some explanation of how charitable remainders are determined, and why the IRS valuation tables are limited to no more than two lives.

Overview of IRC Sec. 664

Although various sections of the tax code recognize charitable contributions (income, gift, estate), there is only one section that specifically addresses CRTs. This is Section 664: *Charitable Remainder Trusts*. It is comprised of about 2,700 statutory words, and is accompanied by approximately 28,000 words of regulations and examples (valuation tables are separate). Section 664 has been a tax law since 1969. Probably because of the influence of wealth on charitable deduction matters, Congress paid little attention to Section 664 until 1997, when it enacted *Taxpayer Relief Act* (P.L. 105-34).

For a quick digest of its scope, Section 664 consists of the following subsections:

(a) General Rule
(b) Character of Distributions
(c) Exemption from Income Taxes

(d)   Definitions; (1) Annuity Trust, (2) Unitrust
(e)   Valuation for Purposes of Charitable Contribution
(f)   Certain Contingencies Permitted

Subsection (a) points out that the tax recognized CRTs are *annuity trusts* and *unitrusts*. Subsection (b) characterizes the distributions to noncharitable recipients as—

(1)   ordinary income (included in the gross income of the annuitant (recipient),
(2)   capital gain (to the extent distributed),
(3)   other income (such as tax exempt income, prior year undistributed income, and depreciation allowances), and
(4)   distribution of trust corpus.

Subsection (c): ***Exemption from Income Taxes***, states—

A charitable remainder annuity trust and a charitable remainder unitrust shall, for any taxable year, not be subject to any tax imposed by this subtitle [Income Taxes], *unless such trust, for such year,* **has unrelated business taxable income.** [Emphasis added.]

"Unrelated business taxable income"? What does this term mean? And at whom is it directed?

It is directed at family-member trustees and administrative agents who, with the advantage of the CRT's tax-exempt status, engage in entrepreneurial competition with ordinary businesses whose income is taxable. This engagement in ordinary business activities (selling goods and services) is one of the more flagrant abuses of CRTs. Moreover, an evangelical and noble-sounding charitable cause can serve as the "perfect diversion" for a flat-out tax evasion scheme.

Charitable Annuity Trusts

Paragraph (A) of Section 664(d)(1) defines a charitable remainder annuity trust as—

*A trust . . . from which a **sum certain** (which is not less than 5 percent nor more than 50 percent of the **initial net fair market value** of all property placed in trust) is to be paid, not less often than annually, to **one or more persons** (at least one of which is not an organization described in section 170(c)* [charitable contribution defined] *and, in the case of individuals, only to an individual who is **living** at the time of the creation of the trust) for a term of years (not in excess of 20 years) **or** for the life or lives of such individual or individuals.* [Emphasis added.]

In other words, a charitable annuity trust is a private contract between a trustor, the government (the IRS), and a charitable institution. The contract must pay a "sum certain" to at least one noncharitable recipient, and must do so for the life of such individual (unless a term certain in years is specified). The "sum certain" is a *stated dollar amount* which is fixed for each periodic payment to the designated individual.

The sum certain is paid first from the income of the trust property. If the income is insufficient, the shortfall is made up from the corpus (principal) of the trust. If the income is greater than the amount needed to pay the sum certain, the excess income is added to the corpus of the trust. Ultimately, the charitable institution will get all of the trust remainders.

A trust is **not** charitable annuity contract if any person has the power to alter the fixed amount payable to the named individual (or individuals). Nor may the fixed amount be paid to other individuals than those so named in the initial trust instrument. The only permissible changes in amounts are payments to the charitable institution itself.

Paragraph (D) of Section 664(d)(1) mandates that the value of the remainder going to charity be—

*at least 10 percent of the initial **net** fair market value of all property placed in trust.*

The term "initial net FMV" means after all transfer tax valuations have been established and reported to the IRS via Form 709: Gift Tax Return.

Form 709 puts the IRS on notice that a charitable remainder trust is being created. The transferred property is described, and all valuations are posted. The IRS has three years to accept or propose changes to the valuations posted by the donor. Regulations require that if the initially transferred property is undervalued, the trust must pay to each recipient, proportionately, the markup difference. If the initial property is overvalued, each recipient must pay back to the trust, proportionately, the markdown difference.

Once the initial transfer of property is made, and its valuation fixed, no additional property can be added to the trust. If the income and corpus become exhausted before the contractual terms are fulfilled, the trust terminates . . . and so does its exempt status.

Charitable Remainder Unitrusts

Section 664(d)(2) defines the characteristics of a charitable remainder unitrust. There are only two differences between a unitrust and an annuity trust. The first difference appears in paragraph (A); the second in paragraph (D) of said section.

Whereas the annuity trust's paragraph (A) uses the term "sum certain," the unitrust's paragraph (A) uses the term: *fixed percentage*. That is, a "fixed percentage" [not less than 5% nor more than 50%] of the initial net FMV is to be paid out no less often than annually. Thus, while the percentage of payment is fixed, the actual dollar amount paid out from a unitrust may vary from year to year. Because of this dollar payout variation, the value of the trust assets must be redetermined at the beginning of each trust accounting year.

The second difference between a unitrust and an annuity trust lies in paragraph (D): valuing the at least 10% charitable remainder interest. Whereas an annuity trust does not recognize any additional contributions of property to the trust, a unitrust **does recognize** additional contributions of property. This is the significance of the following wording in the unitrust's paragraph (D):

> *with respect to each contribution of property to the trust* . . . [the value of such remainder interest shall be determined] . . . *as of the date such property is contributed to the trust.*

By recognizing any additional contributions of property, a unitrust is more flexible than annuity trust. The initial trustor, either by inter vivos (while alive) or testamentary (upon death) transfers can contribute additional property when more facts are known. Presumably, the additional contributions will increase both the noncharitable payouts and the charitable remainders.

To emphasize the differences between an annuity trust (sum certain) and a unitrust (fixed percentage), we present Figure 6.1. Other than the differences portrayed, the mandatory aspects of both types of CRTs are identical.

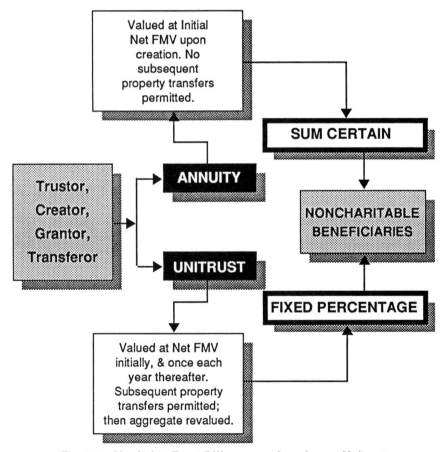

Fig. 6.1 - Charitable Trust Differences: Annuity vs. Unitrust

Mandatory Aspects

An annuity trust must draw down a **fixed dollar sum** each year from the initial property contribution. Correspondingly, a unitrust must draw down a **fixed percentage** of the trust assets, as valued each year. The reason for these fixed amounts is so that the remainder interest that goes to charity can be determined with certainty. This is the basic premise on which all IRS life interest valuation tables are based. If a grantor, trustor, or transferor can distort in any way the fixed sum or fixed percentage of drawdown, the arrangement does not qualify as a charitable remainder trust.

What is left in the trust after the last life-interest recipient dies, must go to charity. That is, there can be no noncharitable remainder interest. The remainder *may* go to charity immediately, at which time the trust terminates. Or, it *may* remain in the trust to be distributed periodically solely for charitable purposes. To emphasize the importance of this remainder concept, we present Figure 6.2. Treatment of the remainder **is the key test** which the IRS uses to ascertain whether a charitable trust qualifies as such.

In theory, two or more noncharitable interests may be involved. In practice, however, two human beings is the limit. Otherwise, there are just too many actuarial variables and uncertainties to be considered. The two lives — called "life interests" — must be in being at the time of creation of the trust. Their drawdowns may be concurrent or consecutive. When payout to the first life ceases, there must be no distortion or diminution of the trust assets. If, for any reason, there is a distortion of the "charitable guarantee," the trust will be disqualified as a charitable remainder.

If more than two individuals are designated as recipients of income, certain distinctions must be made. No more than two persons should be designated as life interests: all others as nonlife interests. Furthermore, triggering events must be specified for terminating the nonlife income. The nonlife-trigger events may include marriage, divorce, birth, or other change in financial status. In no event may a nonlife-ineterest recipient receive income after the death of the last of the two life interests. Keep in mind that the "sum certain" or "fixed percentage" payouts apply to the *combined interests* (life and nonlife) of all noncharitable recipients each year.

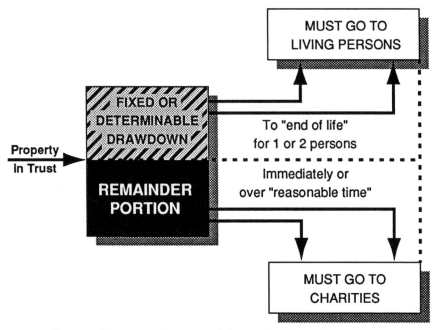

Fig. 6.2 - Mandatory Aspects of Charitable Remainder Trusts

Other restrictions on the trust arrangements apply. For example, a trust will not qualify as a charitable remainder if the noncharitable recipients can be paid the greater (or lesser) of a sum certain or fixed percentage. The recipients must be paid one or the other, without a choice between the two drawdown methods. Once the trust is created irrevocably, it must function as a charitable remainder exclusively . . . from the date of its creation.

Must Avoid Entrepreneurship

Earlier, we quoted part of Section 664(c) which exempts charitable trusts from tax—

. . . unless such trust has unrelated business taxable income.

The phrase "unless such trust has . . ." clearly implies that even an exempt trust can be taxable under certain conditions. The term "unrelated business taxable income" means—

The gross income derived by any [exempt] *organization from any unrelated trade or business . . . regularly carried on by it* [Section 512(a)(1)].

The gist of Section 512 is that a charitable trust may carry on any form of business activity which furthers exclusively its charitable goals. But when the activities veer off into a competitive-type entrepreneurial trade or business, the trust has gone too far. It is attempting to exploit its tax exempt status. Nonexempt businesses pay taxes. If charitable trusts were allowed to compete with tax-paying businesses, it would give said trusts a state-sponsored competitive advantage. Consequently, all forms of trust business activities which are profit-seeking and noncharitable subject the trust to full taxation, just like all other businesses are taxed. Hence, the term "unrelated" means: unrelated to the charitable purposes of the trust.

Section 512 pretty well limits charitable trust activities to those which generate passive income in the form of interest, dividends, capital gains, royalties, mortgage loans, rents from real property, etc. If competitive trade or business activities are engaged in "regularly" (meaning grossing more than $1,000 each taxable year), the trust loses its exempt status.

If a trustor wants the tax benefits of a charitable remainder trust, the trustee **must not exploit** its exempt status. Once he does so, all benefits are retroactively disallowed back to the time when $1,001 in unrelated business income was first generated.

How Remainders Determined

Unless the remainder portion of a trust estate can be determined with certainty, a trust intended as a charitable remainder may not be so. The term "with certainty" means: with reasonable mathematical precision. Estimates, guesses, and waiting for certain events to happen will not do. The moment that any computational uncertainty arises, the charitable remainder characteristic falls aside. When this happens, the tax exempt status of the remainder property is in jeopardy. Fortunately, the IRS publishes its own actuarial tables for establishing the remainder certainty.

Sections 664(d)(**1**)(D) [annuity trusts] and 664(d)(**2**)(D) [unitrusts] state that—

> *the value (**determined under section 7520**) of such remainder interest* [shall be] *at least 10 percent of the net fair market value.* . . . [Emphasis added.]

Obviously, we now have to examine Section 7520.

Section 7520 is titled: **Valuation Tables.** The general rule, subsection (a) states in principal part that—

> *The value of any annuity, any interest for life or a term of years, or **any remainder** or reversionary interest shall be determined—*
>
> > *(1) under tables* [and formulas] *prescribed by the* [IRS], *and*
> > *(2) by using an interest rate (rounded to the nearest 2/10ths of 1 percent) equal to 120 percent of the Federal midterm rate in effect . . . for the month in which the valuation date falls . . .* [or] *for either of the 2 months preceding.*

The first step for determining the remainder value of a CRT is to ascertain the applicable federal interest rate for the month, or either of two prior months, of the valuation. The IRS publishes this information monthly. For example, for the month of March 2000, the midterm interest factor was 8.2%. For the month of August 2000, the midterm rate was 7.6%.

The next step is to procure (from the Government Printing Office) the IRS valuation tables that related to the type of CRT involved. For valuations being made after April 30, 1999, the applicable tables are:

IRS Pub. 1457 — *Actuarial Values, Book Aleph (1999)*
    — for annuity trusts
IRS Pub. 1458 — *Actuarial Values, Book Beth (1999)*
    — for unitrusts
IRS Pub. 1459 — *Actuarial Values, Book Gimel (1999)*
    — for adjustment factors

The tables are based on the latest census mortality data for one and two (single and joint) life-interest recipients. The tables are sophisticated, complex, and extensive (hundreds of pages or more). As such, they are not given away free. They have to be purchased. Otherwise, either the services of a professional actuary are required, or a request to the IRS for a remainder factor ruling can be made. For any of these approaches, a front-end procurement cost is involved. See Figure 6.3 for other steps required.

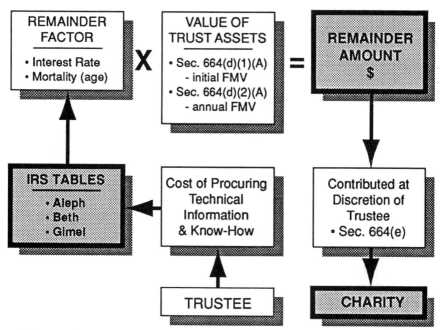

Fig. 6.3 - Steps Required for Determining Remainder Amount to Charity

Tables Include Formulas

In the most fundamental sense possible, the valuation tables are based on three factors. The three factors are: (1) remainder factor, (2) income factor, and (3) annuity factor. Note that the word "factor" is used. Each factor is expressed in five decimal places, such as 0.12345. This attests to the mathematical precision required. The applicable factors are applied to the valuation base of the property in trust at the time the computations are made.

Formula (1) is the remainder factor. It requires the use of a mathematical exponent.

Editorial Note: An "exponent," in case you have forgotten, is a small figure placed above and to the right of another figure to show how many times the latter is to be used as a factor. For example, $b^3 = b \times b \times b$.

The exponent is used in the following inverse form:

(1) Remainder Factor $= \dfrac{1}{(1+i)^t}$

where i = interest rate component
      t = time (mortality) component

Whereas the interest rate component changes monthly, the mortality component changes decennially (every 10 years). As a consequence, the IRS tables are revised after every U.S. census is taken.

To illustrate the precision in remainder factors published by the IRS, we have selected its Table S. The caption to this table reads—

Single Life Remainder Factors
Applicable after April 30, 1999
Based on Life Table 90 CM

The "90 CM" means: 1990 Census Mortality (table).

Table S (the "S" for single life) spans the interest rate range from 4.2% to 14.0%. It spans the life age range from 0 to 109 years. For use-of-table illustration purposes, let us select 8.2% as the interest rate component, and the following ages for the mortality component. Doing so, the remainder factors from Table S are:

Age	Remainder	Age	Remainder
50	0.15855	80	0.56325
60	0.26136	90	0.72694
70	0.39828	100	0.83519

If we were to select age 40, the remainder factor would be 0.09059, or 9%, approximately. This is below the previously stated minimum of *at least 10%* for qualification as a CRT. Hence, for CRT purposes, age 50 (for a remainder of 15.85%) is about the lowest practical age for deriving any worthwhile charitable contribution benefits. On average, it is not until about age 50 that an industrious taxpayer can accumulate sufficient funds for making substantial contributions to charity.

Continuing with presentation of our three formulas, there is Formula (2): the income factor. This is expressed as:

(2) Income Factor = 1.00000 – Remainder Factor

This factor is the drawdown of the trust property by the noncharitable beneficiary (or beneficiaries). For a person at age 70, for example, the income drawdown would be

1.00000 – 0.39828 = 0.60172 or about 60%.

Thus, if $1,000,000 (net FMV) were transferred into a CRT, the life-interest individual would receive (actuarially) about $600,000. Whereupon, some $400,000 would go to charity.

Formula (3) is the annuity factor expressed as follows:

$$(3) \text{ Annuity Factor} = \frac{\text{Income Factor}}{i}$$

where (again) i = interest rate component

Using the example figures above, the annuity factor is 0.60172 ÷ 0.082 = 7.338. Dividing this factor into the $600,000 drawdown, the CRT annuitant would receive an average about $81,766 annually, or about $6,800 per month . . . for life.

Loophole for Abuse

IRC Section 664(e) is titled: ***Valuation for Purposes of Charitable Contribution***. It reads in substantial part—

*For purposes of determining the **amount of any** charitable contribution, the remainder interest . . . **shall be computed on the basis that an amount equal to 5 percent** of the net fair market value of its assets . . . is to be distributed each year.* [Emphasis added.]

Here, a loophole exists. There is no requirement that when the last life beneficiary dies the trust remainder be distributed promptly to charity. The regulations say: "over a reasonable period"; the tax law says: "not in excess of 20 years." What happens if the life beneficiary dies within 30 days — or within five days — of creating the CRT? We have a **true case** to illustrate our point.

The trustor and only life beneficiary was an 84-year-old widow. While on her death bed in a church-sponsored retirement home, she created a unitrust. She had no children, no siblings, and no close relatives. In her will, she had bequeathed 20% of her gross estate to dear friends and 80% to the church where she had been a member for 60 years.

Shortly after moving to the church retirement facility, the 84-year-old had a severe stroke. She recovered to the point where she could partly hear, partly see, and partly sign. Upon learning this, the church attorney, together with the trustor's stock broker and stock broker's attorney prepared a 15-page "standard" charitable remainder unitrust. They did so over a 4-day period.

All of the trustor's assets (stock valued at about $2,285,000) were retitled in the name of the trust. Simultaneously, the church attorney, stock broker, and stock broker's attorney appointed themselves as co-trustees. The trustor obligingly signed all of the "legal papers." Five days later, she died.

The key feature in the trust instrument was its reliance on Section 664(e), cited above. The assets were to be distributed over a period of 12 years, at an annual rate of 8.5%. The arrangement was such that the church got its statutory 5%; the three co-trustees, as "administrators," got 3.5%. The 12-year annuitized value of the initial trust assets amounted to around $5,000,000. Of this, the church would get 60% (12 yrs x 5% per yr) or $3,000,000. The three co-trustees would get $2,000,000! Not a bad fee arrangement for just four days of death-bed legal hustling and intrigue.

7

SURVIVING SPOUSE TRUSTS

> **The First Of Two Married Trustors To Die May Employ A Powerful Tax Benefit Known As: THE MARITAL DEDUCTION: IRC Sec. 2056: "Bequests, Etc. To Surviving Spouse." That Is, The Equity Value Of Property Interests Bequeathed To The Surviving Spouse Is DEDUCTIBLE From The Deceased Spouse's Estate. Those Interests Which Are Deductible, However, Are INCLUDIBLE In The Surviving Spouse's Estate. This Deduction-Inclusion Feature Applies Also To Qualified Terminable Interest Property (Q-TIP) And To Qualifed Domestic Trusts (QDOTs). Special Rules Require The Use Of Schedule M, Form 706.**

Most family trusts start out with a husband and wife, whose combined marital estate is modest to above-modest in wealth amount. As such, each spouse is a separate trustor of his or her own property. Each wants to provide the survivor of the two with an ongoing lifestyle of comfort. In effect, each trustor tries to provide reciprocally for the other, until the end of the survivor's life.

Traditionally, the surviving spouse arrangement goes something like this. A joint inter vivos (while alive) family trust instrument is prepared. Simultaneously, a testamentary instrument (will) is prepared separately for each testator/trustor. The trust is assigned a readily identifiable name, such as the XYZ Family Trust. The "X" representing trustor X (husband); the "Y" representing trustor Y (wife); and the "Z" representing the core family name. The joint trust instrument then dwells on a litany of contingencies and conditions for various trust arrangements (subtrusts, really) when the first trustor dies. The first to die sets the pattern of trusts which the survivor follows.

When the first trustor dies, his portion of the marital estate plus his separate property, if any, are transferred (*net* after transfer taxation) into (usually) three trusts: A, B, and C. All are irrevocable. The "A" is called the Survivor's Trust; the "B" is the Residual Trust; and the "C", if any, is the Disclaimer Trust. Different terms may be assigned to these trusts, depending on the creativity of the joint trust preparer.

In this chapter, we want to focus primarily on Trust A and show how it alone may be one or a combination of three separate surviving spouse subtrusts. We also want to explain the tax laws that motivate each subtrust of A. Trust A is very special. It is functionally a marital deduction trust. For U.S. citizen spouses, the marital deduction is essentially unlimited in amount. Each subtrust A is a *deduction* trust. Being "unlimited" in amount, this one trust arrangement alone could eliminate the decedent spouse's entire transfer tax! Yes, this **is** true.

For a married couple, the same achievement (zero tax) could be attained *without a trust*. The transfer tax laws make no distinction between surviving spouses who have trusts and those who do not have trusts. Thus, obviously, there is much we need to explain to you about surviving spouse arrangements.

The Marital Deduction

The marital deduction is designated in the Tax Code as Section 2056: *Bequests, Etc., to Surviving Spouse.* For many years, this section contained much ambiguous wording. Its ambiguity led to many litigious conflicts between the IRS and executors of decedent spouses' estates. Disputes invariably arose because of "formula bequests" that sought the maximum marital deduction allowable. The formulas were directed at such statutory wordings as—

The aggregate amount of the deduction allowed . . . shall not exceed the greater of—
(i) $250,000 or

(ii)   50 percent of the value of the adjusted gross estate [of the decedent spouse].

In 1981, this and other ambiguous wording were repealed. For spouses dying after 1981, the marital deduction law, general rule, now reads as—

*(a)   **Allowance of Marital Deduction** — For purposes of the tax imposed by section 2001* [the death transfer tax], *the value of the taxable estate, except as limited by subsection (b), **shall be determined by deducting** from the value of the gross estate an amount equal to the value of **any interest in property** which passes or has passed from the decedent to the surviving spouse, **but only to the extent that** such interest is included in determining the value of the gross estate.* [Emphasis added.]

This Section 2056(a) is now referred to as the "unlimited" marital deduction. It is unlimited in dollar amount, though there are some restrictions on the *types* of property interests that can be deducted.   The restrictions are classed as *terminable interest property*, which we'll explain later.

Except for terminable interest property, whatever the decedent spouse bequests to (or gifts to) his surviving spouse is deductible. Whatever amount is deducted from the decedent spouse's gross estate, his taxable estate is reduced correspondingly. If his gross estate is $5,000,000, for example, he can bequest deductibly $1,000,000, $3,000,000 . . . or whatever. As you'll see immediately below, certain tax reality precautions are required.   Shifting everything to one's surviving spouse is not the best strategy.

Includible in Survivor's Estate

Is there a "catch" in the unlimited marital deduction rule? Of course there is. Isn't there always?

Stated simply, whatever property interests are deductible from the decedent spouse's estate **are includible** in the surviving spouse's estate. This is the significance of that clause in Section 2056(a) which reads—

property which passes [at time of death] *or has passed* [prior to death, by gift] *from the decedent to the surviving spouse* . . .

Section 2056(a) was never intended to be an absolute tax freebie. It is not an outright exclusion; it is a **conditional deduction**. The condition is that, whatever amount is deducted from the gross estate of the first spouse to die, is included in the gross estate of the surviving spouse. In other words, it is transfer taxed in the estate of one spouse or the other. Such is the significance of the last clause in Section 2053(a)—

. . . *but only to the extent that such interest is included in determining the value of the gross estate.*

Which gross estate? The decedent spouse's gross estate or the surviving spouse's gross estate? The answer is: both. The tax theory is that one spouse or the other will pay the transfer tax on the deductible property interests. For visualization purposes, we portray this deduction-inclusion concept in Figure 7.1. Note that we also show the statutory exclusions (exemption credits) for each spouse. These statutory exclusions (usually the genesis of an exempt subtrust) are not affected by the marital deduction process.

As we try to show in Figure 7.1, by virtue of Section 2056(a): *Allowance of Marital Deduction,* a decedent spouse could bequeath his entire gross estate to his surviving spouse. Were he to do so, his estate would pay no death tax. The surviving spouse's estate would pay maximum death tax. Rarely is this a good strategy. For the decedent spouse, there are administrative expenses; there may be encumbrances upon the bequeathed property; there may be outstanding debts and claims against the decedent; the statutory exclusion (covered in Chapter 3) could be "thrown away"; and the surviving spouse may not live very long after the decedent spouse dies. Many factors need to be considered before arbitrarily passing deductible property to one's spouse.

Realistically, only three factors need be considered. One is the difference in likely death tax rates between the two spouses. It is always advisable to shift property from a high tax rate spouse to the lower tax rate spouse. The second consideration is the gap in life

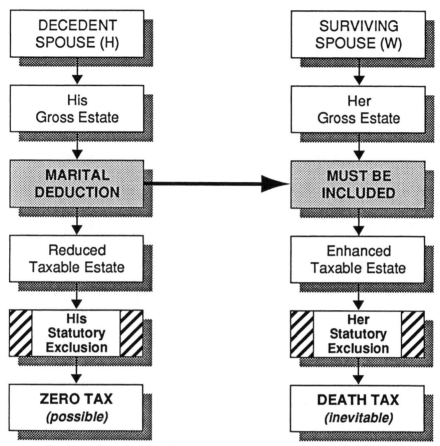

Fig. 7.1 - Effect of Marital Deduction on Surviving Spouse's Estate

expectancy between the two spouses. If the surviving spouse lives significantly long, there is opportunity for direct consumption and gifting away some of the marital deduction property, before the survivor dies. Any prior-to-death consumption/gifting reduces the adverse tax consequences to the surviving spouse. The third consideration is the likely change in value of the property (up or down) after the decedent spouse dies.

Upon death of the surviving spouse, there is no additional marital deduction (assuming, of course, that no remarriage has taken place). To the extent that the marital deduction property has not been consumed by the surviving spouse, it is transfer taxed upon her death. This holds true whether there is a survivor's trust or no survivor's trust. In the full citation of Section 2056(a) above, was the word "trust" ever mentioned? No, it was not. A marital deduction trust is an administrative convenience: not a tax requirement.

Deductible Interests Defined

Section 2056(a) within itself provides no clear distinction of which property interests are deductible and which are not. The nearest indicator is the clause: *except as limited by subsection (b)* [of Section 2056]. Section 2056(b) is very complicated. Less complicated is Regulation § 20.2056(a)–2(b): *Deductible interests*. Selected citations from this regulation are instructive.

Accordingly, paragraph (1) of this regulation reads—

Any property item which passed from the decedent to his surviving spouse is a "nondeductible interest" to the extent it is not included in the decedent's gross estate.

The rationale here is that, if the property item is not included on Form 706 in the asset schedules A through I, there is nothing to deduct. If the property item had been sold to, or exchanged with, the surviving spouse, or to/with some other person or family member for "full and adequate" consideration, it is not a required inclusion on Form 706.

There is a self-policing twist to this regulation. To claim the marital deduction, each property item must be described on Schedule M (Form 706). This deduction schedule is titled: *Bequests, etc., to Surviving Spouse* (identical with the title of Section 2056). Schedule M requires that the following information be listed:

- Item number of the property listed on Schedules A through I.
- Additional description of the property interest(s) intended for passing to spouse.

- Amount of expenses and indebtedness deducted on other schedules for same property.
- Equity amount in dollars passing to surviving spouse.

Paragraphs (2) and (3) of Regulation § 20.2056(a)–2(b) treat property expenses, indebtedness, taxes, and losses (casualties and thefts) as nondeductible items. These items are allowed as separate deductions on Schedules J, K, and L of Form 706. No double deductions (on any tax form) are ever allowed. Hence, the amounts on Schedules J, K, and L must be subtracted out before listing an item on Schedule M. For example, a property item market valued at $500,000 with a mortgage of $150,000 would be listed on Schedule M at $350,000. It is the equity value, not the full market value, that passes.

And, finally, paragraph (4) of the above regulation states—

A property interest passing to a decedent's surviving spouse which is a "terminable interest" . . . is a nondeductible interest to the extent specified in [subsection (b) of Section 2056].

What is a "terminable interest"? We explain below.

Terminable Interest Property

Regulation § 20.2056(b)–1(b) states—

A "terminable interest" in property is an [ownership] *interest which will terminate or fail on the lapse of time or on the occurrence or the failure to occur of some contingency. Life estates, terms for years, annuities, patents, and copyrights are therefore terminable interests. A contractual obligation, the discharge of which would not have the effect of an annuity or a term for years, is not a terminable interest.*

Stated another way, a property interest which passes directly to someone else upon a surviving spouse's death is a terminable interest. It is "terminable" in that the predecedent spouse has directed the property elsewhere than into the surviving spouse's estate. Were such an arrangement allowed as a marital deduction, it would escape transfer taxation altogether. Obviously, therefore, terminable interest property is **not deductible** (as a marital deduction) under Section 2056. A depiction of such an arrangement is presented in Figure 7.2. Compare with Figure 7.1.

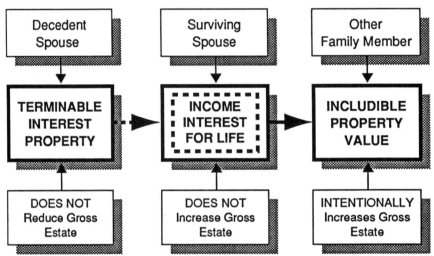

Fig. 7.2 - The Effect on Surviving Spouse of Terminable Interest Property

Subsection 2056(a): *Allowance of Marital Deduction*, employs the clause . . . *except as limited by subsection (b)* . . . . Subsection (b) is titled: *Limitation in the Case of Life Estate or Other Terminable Interest*. Whereas subsection (a) consists of about 70 words, subsection (b) consists of about 2,000 words!

The best we can do here is to cite the captions of the enumerated paragraphs that are prescribed by subsection (b). Accordingly, said paragraphs are:

(1) *General Rule* — no deduction allowed.
(2) *Interest in Unidentified Assets* — no deduction unless identified on Schedule M of Form 706.
(3) *Interest of Spouse Conditioned on Survival for Limited Period* — allowable if a common disaster occurs, or if surviving spouse deceases within 6 months of predecedent spouse.

(4) *Valuation of Interest Passing to Surviving Spouse* — amount when allowed subject to reduction by allocable portion of transfer tax, encumbrances, and indebtedness.

(5) *Life Estate with Power of Appointment in Surviving Spouse* — if said power can be exercised only by surviving spouse, then the property interest is allowable under subsection (a).

(6) *Life Insurance or Annuity Payments with Power of Appointment in Surviving Spouse* — same as (5) above.

(7) *Election with Respect to Life Estate for Surviving Spouse* — **more on this below**.

(8) *Special Rule for Charitable Remainder Trusts* — allowable if surviving spouse is the only noncharitable beneficiary.

(9) *Denial of Double Deduction* — only one deduction either during life or upon death of predecedent spouse.

Except for paragraph (7), the gist of all of the above is that no marital deduction is allowed for terminable interest property. There are certain exceptions, yes. The exceptions relate to powers of appointment, simultaneous (or near-simultaneous) deaths, and charitable remainders.

The QTIP Election

Section 2056(b)(7) is a special rule that is exercisable after death by the decedent spouse's executor. It is called: the QTIP election" The acronym QTIP stands for: Qualified Terminable Interest Property (pronounced as Q-TIP). It is an *election* rule. This means that it must be chosen, and so designated in writing, at the appropriate time. The appropriate time may be when filing Form 709: Gift Tax Return, and/or Form 706: Death Tax Return.

The most advantageous appropriate time is after death of the decedent spouse, when the gross estate is being inventoried and valued. At that time, the executor is in the best position to judge whether the marital deduction is helpful or not. If the executor feels that a marital deduction is helpful, he elects to include the QTIP property into the decedent spouse's estate. From the decedent's estate, the QTIP property automatically passes to the surviving spouse's estate. In such estate, the QTIP property is subsequently transfer taxed.

Selected portions of paragraph (7) of subsection (b) read—

*In the case of [QTIP] property, in which the surviving spouse has a qualifying income interest for life, . . such property [upon election] shall be treated as passing to the surviving spouse, and . . . no part of such property shall be treated as passing to any person other than the surviving spouse. . . . An election under this paragraph with respect to **any property** shall be made by the executor on the return of tax imposed by [Form 706]. Such an election, once made, shall be irrevocable.*

How does the decedent spouse's executor make the QTIP election? By carefully reading the instructions in the head portion of Schedule M (Form 706): **Bequests, etc., to Surviving Spouse.**

The pertinent instructions are identified as: **Election to Deduct Qualified Terminable Interest Property under Section 2056(b)(7).** In pertinent part, these instructions read—

*If a trust (or other property) meets the [QTIP] requirements under section 2056(b)(7) and . . . is entered in whole or in part as a deduction on Schedule M, then unless the executor specifically identifies the trust (or other property) to be excluded from the election, the executor **shall be deemed** to have made an election . . . under section 2056(b)(7).* [Emphasis added.]

In other words, identify the QTIP property for which the election is made, and enter it as a deduction on Schedule M. Once this is done by the predecedent's spouse's executor, the burden is on the surviving spouse's executor to include the deducted amount in the surviving spouse's gross estate upon her demise.

The Alien Spouse Rule

Generally, the marital deduction is not allowed where the surviving spouse is not a U.S. citizen at the time of the decedent spouse's death. This is so prescribed by Section 2056(d): *Disallowance of Marital Deduction where Surviving Spouse not U.S. Citizen.* Paragraph (1) of subsection (d) states clearly that—

> *Except as provided in paragraph (2), if the surviving spouse of the decedent is not a citizen of the U.S.—*
> *(A) no deduction shall be allowed under subsection (a), and*
> *(B) section 2040(b) shall not apply.*

Section 2040(b): What does this refer to? It is titled: *Certain Joint Interests of Husband and Wife.*

On its face, Section 2040(b) makes no distinction between U.S. surviving spouses and alien surviving spouses. It says that only one-half of the value of a qualified joint interest (tenants by the entirety or joint tenants with right of survivorship) needs to be included in the decedent spouse's estate. Subsection 2056(d)(1)(B) takes precedence over Section 2040(b) by mandating that . . . *section 2040(b) shall not apply.*

Now what? This is where paragraph (2) of Section 2056(d) comes into play. Paragraph (2) is captioned: *Marital Deduction Allowed for Certain Transfers in Trust*, and says—

> *(A) Paragraph (1) shall not apply to any property passing to the surviving spouse in a **qualified domestic trust** [QDOT] . . .*
> *(B) If such property is transferred to such a trust, or is irrevocably assigned [thereto], before the date on which [Form 706 is filed].* [Emphasis added.]

Meanwhile, paragraph (3) permits the decedent spouse to direct that the alien surviving spouse's estate include any maritally deducted property. Paragraph (4) says that paragraph (1) shall not apply where the alien spouse becomes a U.S. citizen and resident before the decedent spouse's Form 706 is filed.

Qualified Domestic Trust Defined

International marriages are common these days. Such marriages, however, do create transfer tax problems because of jurisdictional disputes over property owned by foreign citizens. Prior to 1987, alien spouses married to U.S. citizens were simply not recognized for marital deduction purposes under Section 2056. The Tax Reform Act of 1986 introduced a new section to the Tax Code, namely: Section 2056A: *Qualified Domestic Trust.*

As Section 2056A now stands, it consists of approximately 2,500 statutory words. It is accompanied by about 15,000 regulatory words. Obviously, all we can do is touch on some of its highlights. For example, we have to point out to you that certain security arrangements must be made, to assure that the transfer tax on the maritally transferred property is accounted for and paid. For this purpose, there is **Form 706-QDT**: *U.S. Estate Tax Return for Qualified Domestic Trusts* that has to be addressed.

Subsection (a) of Section 2056A defines the term "qualified domestic trust" as—

With respect to any decedent, any trust if the trust instrument—

(A) requires that at least 1 trustee be an individual citizen of the U.S. or a domestic corporation, and
(B) provides that no distribution [of property] *may be made from the trust unless a trustee* [in subparagraph (A)] *has the right to withhold from such distribution the* [transfer] *tax imposed by this section on such distribution.*

The term "any decedent" refers to whichever spouse, U.S. or alien, seeks the marital deduction benefits. The term "any trust" refers to any domestic or foreign trust into which intended marital deduction property has been transferred. And, further, "such trust" must meet the regulatory provisions for ensuring collection of the transfer tax, and for which the executor for the decedent has authority to make a qualified election. When such trust is qualified (for the marital deduction), it is acronymed as a QDOT: Qualified DOmestic Trust (pronounced Q-DOT).

IRS Regulations require that QDOTs post a security bond or other equivalent to ensure the collection of tax. If the trust assets exceed $2,000,000, the surety arrangement must cover at least 65% of those assets. If the assets are equal to or less than $2,000,000, assurance must be given that no more than 35% of such assets will be in real estate outside of the U.S. For purposes of the $2,000,00 threshold, a personal residence (primary *plus* secondary) *exclusion* up to $600,000 is allowed. The presumption is that one residence may be in the U.S., while the other is in a foreign country.

Whenever the personal residence exclusion is claimed, or whenever there are property interests in partnerships or corporations, or whenever there is foreign real property involved, an annual statement is required. Such is the purpose of Form 706-QDT. This is a 4-page form with six pages of instructions. The form computes the tax on distributions from the QDOT corpus; indicates whether the alien spouse has become a U.S. citizen; and designates the value of the QDOT property on the date of the surviving spouse's death. The form also requires the summarization of all prior and current taxable distributions, all property remaining in QDOTs, and all marital and charitable deductions.

Making the QDOT Election

Because of the annual requirements of Form 706-QDT, the QDOT election must be made within one year of the *last annual* Form 706-QDT. The "last annual" such form means upon death of that spouse who is claiming the marital deduction on his or her regular Form 706.

The QDOT election is made simply by listing the entire trust assets on Schedule M (Form 706) and deducting its value. An instruction to this effect appears on Schedule M under the caption: *Election to Deduct Qualified Domestic Trust Property under Section 2056A.* In pertinent part, this instruction reads—

If a trust meets the requirements . . . under Section 2056A(a) and this return is filed no later than 1 year after the time prescribed . . ., and the entire value of the trust or trust property is entered as a deduction on Schedule M, then unless the executor specifically identifies the trust to be excluded from the election, the executor shall be deemed to have made an election to have the entire trust as qualified domestic trust property. [Emphasis added.]

When compared to a QTIP election, there is a QDOT "catch." No partial elections are allowed. This is the significance of the emphasized terms above: *entire value* [of] *entire trust*. This feature precludes any covert tax avoidance by a surviving spouse who may not be residing in the U.S. subsequent to the decedent spouse's death. Once made, the election is irrevocable.

Schedule M Summarized

At this point, we have covered three forms of marital deductions. There is (1) ordinary marital deduction property (may be in trust or not), (2) the QTIP trust (terminable interest property), and (3) the QDOT trust (alien spouse with foreign assets likely). We class all of these as "surviving spouse trusts" because they take advantage of the marital deduction benefits on Schedule M: *Bequests, etc., to Surviving Spouse*. These listings and other related information are entered on Schedule M. For instructional coverage on surviving spouse trusts, we need to summarize Schedule M for you.

A functional diagram of Schedule M is presented in Figure 7.3. Note that the upper portion of Schedule M addresses the QTIP and QDOT elections. These deemed elections are followed by three "Yes-No" type questions. The first such question is—

1. *Did any property pass to the surviving spouse as a result of a qualified disclaimer?* ☐ *Yes,* ☐ *No. If "Yes", attach a copy of the written disclaimer required by section 2518(b)* [Qualified Disclaimer Defined].

A disclaimer is the process of disinheriting an interest in property that otherwise would pass to the disclaimant and be included in his or her gross estate. When disclaimed, the property passes automatically to the next heir in line. Where the surviving spouse is the "next heir," the property often is identified in a separate Disclaimer Trust. The disclaimed trust property is not deductible on Schedule M, but is indicated thereon as a reminder to the surviving spouse to include said property in her gross estate.

Sched. M	BEQUESTS, ETC. TO SURVIVING SPOUSE		
☐ The QTIP Election ☐ The QDOT Election			

Specific Questions		Yes	No
1. Prior disclaimers ---------------------			
2. Spousal citizenship --------------------			
3. Joint annuities ---------------------------			

Item	Description of Marital Deduction Property	Value
//// Total amount of property interests ➡		
Transfer & other succession taxes payable out of property interests above.	• Federal	////
	• State	////
	• Foreign	////
//// Add the above & subtract from total		< >
NET AMOUNT OF DEDUCTIBLE PROPERTY INTERESTS		☐

Fig. 7.3 - General Format of Schedule M, Form 706

Question **2** on Schedule M consists of five subquestions, as follows:

a. *In what country was the surviving spouse born?*_____
b. *What is the surviving spouse's date of birth?*_____
c. *Is the surviving spouse a U.S. Citizen?* ☐ *Yes,* ☐ *No*
d. *If the surviving spouse is a naturalized citizen, when did* [such] *spouse acquired citizenship?*_____
e. *If the surviving spouse is not a U.S. citizen, of what country is* [such] *spouse a citizen?*_____

Obviously, the citizenship of the surviving spouse has an important bearing on the validity of the property listings on Schedule M.

Question **3** is captioned: *Election Out of QTIP Treatment of Annuities*. ☐ Yes, ☐ No. This question relates to joint and survivor annuities where there are significant mortality differences between husband and wife. An annuity, by contract, is terminable interest property. By **not** electing out of the QTIP election (answering "No"), the decedent spouse gets a deduction for the surviving spouse's annuity amount. When the surviving spouse dies, any ongoing annuity value is generally zero. In other words, there is no inclusion in the surviving spouse's estate (when she dies).

The bottom portion of Figure 7.3 directs that all marital deduction property interests be totaled. From this total, if there are insufficient other funds for doing so, some transfer taxes may be payable from the property listed on Schedule M. When so paid, said taxes reduce the final amount of the marital deduction that is allowable.

When Surviving Spouse Dies

Suppose a surviving spouse lives 5, 10, 15, or more years after the death of the predeceased spouse. What happens when the surviving spouse dies? Is there any way that the IRS keeps track of the marital deduction property on Schedule M of the predeceased spouse's Form 706?

Not really. The IRS relies more on the honor system than it probably cares to acknowledge. It relies solely on the administrative ability of the **executor** of the surviving spouse's estate to resurrect the remnants of the predeceased spouse's Schedule M and incorporate those property interests into the surviving spouse's gross estate. In other words, by virtue of Code Section 2002: *Liability for Payment*, the IRS holds the executor's feet to the fire. This 12-word section reads—

The tax imposed by this chapter [Chapter 11 – Estate Tax] *shall be paid by the executor.*

We portray in Figure 7.4 the end effect of Section 2002.

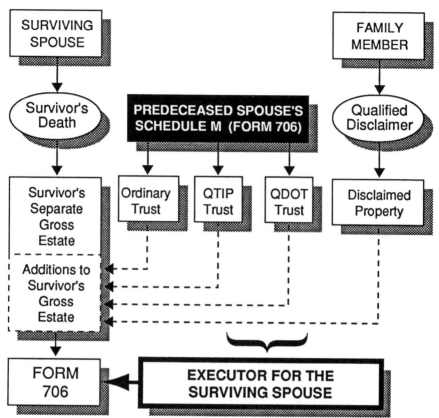

Fig. 7.4 - Liability of Surviving Spouse's Executor for Estate Accounting

As brutal as this liability may sound, the executor of the surviving spouse's estate does get some helpful reminders among the general questions asked on *every* decedent's Form 706. Toward this end, there are four particular hint-type questions.

The foremost hint-question appears on page 2 of Form 706 at the caption: *Marital status of the decedent at time of death—*

☐ *Widow or widower – Name, SSN, and date of death of predeceased spouse* ▶ _____.

This question should alert the executor to seek out a copy of the prior spouse's Form 706.

The next hint-question (on page 2) is—

Does the gross estate contain any . . . QTIP property from a prior gift or estate? ☐ *Yes,* ☐ *No. If "Yes", these assets must be shown on Schedule F* [Other Miscellaneous Property].

The third hint-question appears on page 3 as—

Were there in existence at the time of the decedent's death:
a. Any trusts created by the decedent during his or her lifetime? ☐ *Yes,* ☐ *No.*
b. Any trusts not created by the decedent under which the decedent possessed any power, beneficial interest, or trusteeship? ☐ *Yes,* ☐ *No.*

If "Yes" to either part of this question, the trustee or successor trustee must provide a description of the property interests that are includible in the surviving spouse's gross estate.

The fourth and final hint-question for our purposes on Form 706 (page 3) is—

*Was the decedent **ever** the beneficiary of a trust for which **a deduction** was claimed by the estate of a predeceased spouse . . . and which **is not** reported on this return?* ☐ *Yes,* ☐ *No. If "Yes", attach an explanation.* [Emphasis added.]

In anticipation of this "ever" question relating to prior marital property deductions, the most credible attachment is a copy of the predeceased spouse's Schedule M. In reality, though, retrieving such schedule may be difficult. Much depends on the record-keeping discipline of the family structure, the lapse of time between the two spousal deaths, and whether the surviving spouse remarried to become a second Schedule M beneficiary. Because of such difficulties, our position is that every Form 706 and every Schedule M should be made a permanent part of the records of every stalwart family . . . with or without a trust.

8

DESIRABLE TRUST FEATURES

> Typically, Family Trust Agreements Run About
> 35 Pages. Fully 25 Of These Are Standard
> Clauses And Powers Which Can Be Relegated
> To An Appendix. Most Of The Forepart Of The
> Contract Addresses How The Trustors Treat
> Their Own Property While Alive. Only A Few
> Pages Address The Distribution Of Trust
> Income And Principal To Successor
> Beneficiaries Over A Period Of 10, 20, Or 30
> Years. More Desirable Features Include Better
> Documentation Of Property Values, Contem-
> plation Of Termination Events, The Naming Of
> Family Trustees, The Importance Of A Will,
> And The Clarification Of "Creation" Dates.

We all make mistakes of one kind or another throughout life. So long as the mistakes are discovered during life, they are correctable . . . or at least not likely to be repeated. In the case of family trust instruments, however, whatever mistakes are made are "cast in concrete" once the trustors are deceased. Trying subsequently to correct any alleged mistakes is costly, time consuming, and inevitably leads to disputes between family members and their professional advisors.

There seems to be one common mistake that all trustors make. Once they decide upon creating a family trust, they dash off to a trust preparer, usually an attorney, to have "all documents" prepared. The attorney prepares a 35-page treatise (plus or minus a few pages), much of which is boilerplated from previous family trust instruments that he, his colleagues, or his law firm have prepared. Rarely are more than one or two pages tailored to the particular family situation that the trustors seek to address. Rather than being a flexible roadmap for the distributions of income and corpus to designated family members, the trust instrument is tailored to the legal system in the state where the trustors are domiciled. When push comes to shove, it is the "legal system" — not the surviving family members — that benefits most from family trust arrangements.

Family trust instruments tend to be complex, obfuscating, and inflexible. Because of this, we want to present in this chapter some useful guidelines that you as a trustor may pursue when instructing your trust preparer what you want prepared. Our approach is to have you think ahead 10 years or so **beyond your grave** and critique what your family and their advisors are doing with your trust property. Looking ahead is not an easy task, yet it is doable when based on other family trust experiences where mistakes have been made. Our goal here is to outline what we think are desirable trust features — some "do's and don'ts" — you might insist on, when finalizing your estate affairs.

Don't Bypass a Will

It is easy to get caught up in the euphoria and mystique of family trusts. In the process, many trustors overlook the stand-alone importance of a will. They succumb to the wishes of the trust preparer who wants to combine the will and the trust into one document. The result is a "will-trust" which we caution against.

Functionally and chronologically, a will serves a different purpose from that of a trust. Upon death, a will serves as a transitional document for identifying property and heirs, and for focusing on the preparation and filing of Form 706: *U.S. Estate* [Death] *Tax Return*. Transitionally, a will also enables a trustor's personally appointed executor to clear the residual estate of family memorabilia, unmarketable items (the "pots and pans"), low-marketable items (under $1,000 or so each), and nontrust-desired items (such as used vehicles, equipment, furniture, fixtures, etc.). Whereas the administration of a will may take from six to 18 *months* (sometimes longer), the administration of a trust may take anywhere from five to 50 *years* (often shorter). Consequently, it is helpful to view the administrative end of a will as the administrative beginning of a trust.

Promoters of will-trusts foster the idea that your executor and trustee can be one and the same person. Yes, this is possible, But it is like wearing two different hats at the same time. Much self-discipline and special focus are required so as not to confuse the two different tasks. An executor focuses on inventorying, valuing, distributing, and *settling* a decedent's estate. A trustee focuses on managing income-producing property for ongoing periods of time **after** an estate is settled. As we depict in Figure 8.1, the executor functions come first, and are separate and apart from the trustee functions. Trust administration does not begin until there is an acceptance letter from the IRS concerning estate Form 706.

IRS "Acceptance Letter"

To help your executor perform his or her duties properly, as testator/trustor you should set forth in your will three special *pretrust* (P/T) directives. These directives are in addition to the regular inclusions in any will. The nature and purpose of said directives are to:

P/T 1 — Rid the estate of all personal effects, memorabilia, "pots and pans," and items of nil and low market value. Estimate their values for Form 706 purposes, but otherwise clear them out of the estate.

P/T 2 — Make direct bequests to all nontrust beneficiaries, if any, and make "advance payments" to needy trust beneficiaries. Do so up to the statutory exclusion amount claimed on Form 706. These distributions are tax free to the recipients. They'll love it!

P/T 3 — Convert the bulk of the taxable portion of the estate to income-producing property, if not already in such form. If in such form, identify it for specific conveyance to the trust.

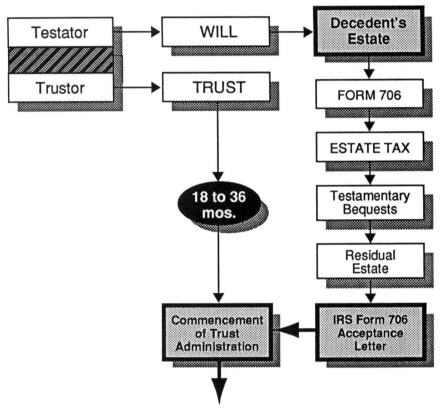

Fig. 8.1 - The Role of a Will as Predecessor to a Trust

Our position is that a decedent trustor's estate is not settled until the executor receives from the IRS a closing letter titled: *Acceptance of Estate Tax Return*. We first brought this to your attention back on page 3-20. Said letter is not forthcoming until all adjustments to Form 706, if any, are agreed to. Then the "acceptance" reads in part—

> *This letter is evidence that the Federal tax return for the estate has either been accepted as filed or has been accepted after an adjustment to which you have agreed. You should keep this letter as a permanent record. . . . This letter and proof of payments, such as cancelled checks or receipts, will establish that your personal liability for the tax **has been settled**.*

This IRS letter ends the estate, and starts the trust. It is a one-page document. A copy should be made part of the trust records.

Confusion over Forms 1041

Ordinarily, it takes about a year after the filing of Form 706 for the IRS to issue an acceptance letter. If there are valuation disputes or other adjustments to Form 706, it can take up to three years. Thus, generally, there is about an 18- to 36-month spread between the date of death of a trustor and the settlement of his or her estate. During this time, income is produced by those assets held in the estate.

When an estate (or trust) produces a gross income of $600 or more for a given accounting year, an income tax return is required. Such is the purpose of **Form 1041**: *U.S. Income Tax Return for Estates and Trusts*. Here, now, emerges true confusion between wills, estates, and trusts. This confusion pervades every family trust arrangement where the role of a will is suppressed and downplayed in preference to the excitement of formulating the trust instrument. The income of an estate **and** of a trust cannot be filed on the same Form 1041. Let us explain.

In order to report the income of an estate, your executor must apply to the IRS for a Tax I.D., called: EIN (Employer Identification Number). **Form SS-4** is used for this purpose. Said EIN has nothing to do with whether the estate engages employees or not. The EIN is an IRS account number only. It is similar to an individual's SSN (social security number) used on Forms 1040.

Form 1041 is so designed that its duration of applicability is indicated by checkboxes: *Initial return* ☐, *Final return* ☐, etc. There is also a checkbox for indicating: *Decedent's estate* ☐. Thus, for estates, Form 1041 is required only for the period of time from date of death to settlement of the estate.

Confusion arises because the decedent's trust also requires a Tax I.D. — an EIN. The trust EIN is a SEPARATE EIN from that of the estate. This means that a separate application Form SS-4 must be filed. When the trust first generates $600 or more in gross income, it indicates this to the IRS by checking the box: *Initial return* ☐. The trustee must also indicate on Form 1041 whether the trustor has created a *Simple trust* ☐, or a *Complex trust* ☐. There are significant differences between the two. We'll explain the differences in Chapter 11: Comprehending Form 1041.

Attorneys and legal firms (and CPA firms, too) are not noted for the clarity of instructions to their clients. What generally happens is this. When the trustor dies, the executor/trustee reports such fact to the trust preparer (or to some other attorney) to "get things started." Immediately, the attorney or his paralegal assistant applies for a trust EIN. When the trust EIN is issued, an attorney-client (or a CPA-client) account is set up, whereupon the billing-for-services process starts. The billing will go on, month after month, until the trust terminates . . . years later.

What about the estate EIN?

That's another matter. Applying for the estate EIN is a task for the executor to pursue. An inexperienced and uninformed executor/trustee can so easily get confused. Without proper instructions to the contrary, the trust EIN is used for estate EIN purposes. To make matters even worse, the payers of income to the estate, when not informed of the EIN, file their "information returns" (the Forms 1099, etc.) with the deceased trustor's SSN. Before long, the inattention to tax identifying details snowballs into one dreadful IRS computer-matching mess.

Here's what we are trying to warn you about. Do not prematurely engage in trust administration until all estate administration matters are settled. For guidance in this regard, we present Figure 8.2. For best administration of the estate **and** of the trust, instructions along the lines of Figure 8.2 — or an improved diagram thereof — could be incorporated into, or as a supplement to, both the will instrument and the trust instrument.

Clarifying Creation Dates

Every trust instrument starts with preamble wording that states the names of the trustors, the initial trustees, and the name and date of creation of the family trust. The particular words used follow the format and style of the trust preparer's own choosing. There is an air of contractual formality, which indeed there should be. The document is formally labeled—

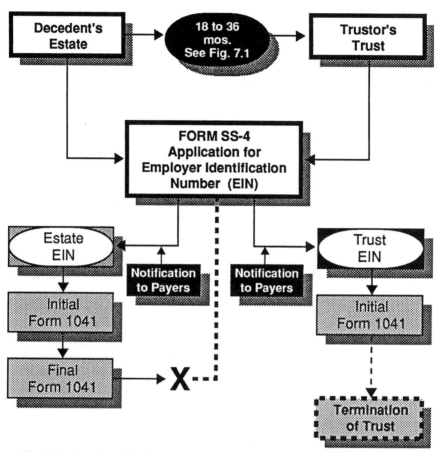

Fig. 8.2 - The Need for Two Separate EINs and Two Separate Forms 1041

DECLARATION OF FAMILY TRUST

. . . or other equivalent title words.

For example, using purely fictitious names, the preamble wording might read as—

JOHN J. JONES, Husband, and MARY M. JONES, Wife, called the "Trustors" and the "Trustees" depending on the context, declare that by this Agreement they hereby create the JONES FAMILY 2002 TRUST, which is entered into on ___(date)___ as set forth hereinafter.

The date entered above is that on which the completed instrument is executed and witnessed. On page 35 or thereabouts, the signatures authenticating the trust contract appear as—

IN WITNESS WHEREOF, the Trustors and Trustees have executed this Agreement on the ____20th____ day of __September,__ 2002.

/s/_____   /s/_____
      JOHN J. JONES,   *JOHN J. JONES,*
         Trustor   *Trustee*

/s/_____   /s/_____
      MARY M. JONES,   *MARY M. JONES,*
         Trustor   *Trustee*

The signatures are witnessed on the same date as that entered above.

> *Editorial Note*: When you see the same name as trustor and trustee, you know that the trust instrument is a revocable document. When you see husband and wife, both as trustors and as trustees, you know that there are **two** revocable trust instruments. When one spouse dies, that spouse's trust instrument becomes irrevocable. When the surviving spouse dies, the two independent trusts combine and become irrevocable. At this point, the family trust is created.

Here comes the creation date problem . . . and its clarification. When the first trustor dies, Form 1041 for his *estate* asks for: *Date entity created_____*. Which date is entered? The date of executing the trust instrument or the date of death of the first decedent trustor?

Answer: The date of death of the first decedent trustor.

When the first decedent trustor's estate is settled (as evidenced by the IRS's Form 706 acceptance letter), what date is used on Form 1041 (*Date entity created*) for the first decedent's *trust*? Is it the formal contract date of "In Witness Whereof"?

Answer: No. It is the day following the date on the IRS acceptance letter. Unfortunately, there is a time lag of about 18 months. So, use reasonable discretion.

When the surviving trustor dies, the "Date entity created" likewise appears on that decedent's estate Form 1041. The proper date, of course, is the date of the surviving trustor's death.

When the surviving trustor's estate is settled (as evidenced by an entirely separate IRS acceptance letter), what date is entered on the *family trust* Form 1041 for "Date entity created"?

Answer: The family trust is created on the day following the date on which the surviving trustor's estate is settled.

Yes, the various "creation dates" can be confusing. They need not be, if your executor/trustee has adequate tax return preparation counseling. Simply follow the natural sequence of human events as each trustor dies. Do not be misled by the legal jargon of the trust instrument creation.

Declare Trustor's Intent Early

Following the contract preamble, the terms, conditions, and distributive intent of the trustors starts getting garbled. It is as though the trust preparer, his firm, and his associates are deliberately trying to discourage the trustors (and their successor trustees) from reading the trust instrument and trying to understand it.

Here's a prime example of what we mean. The following true paragraph is lifted directly from a living trust document recently executed in the State of California. It reads—

It is the Trustors' intention that the Trustee shall have no more extensive power over any community property transferred to the Trust Estate than either of the trustors would have had under California Civil Code Sections 5125 and 5127 had this Trust not been created, and this instrument shall be interpreted to achieve this objective. This limitation shall terminate on the death of either Trustor. Any separate property transferred to this Trust shall remain the separate property of the contributing Trustor and during joint lifetimes of both Trustors. The non-contributing Trustor shall acquire no rights or interests in said property other than rights to manage the property in a fiduciary capacity under the terms of this Agreement. The provisions of California Civil Code Section 5110.150 shall apply to this trust and property transferred to the trust which originated in a joint tenancy form of record title between the Trustors is hereby expressly agreed by the Trustors to have originated in and to be community property unless expressly referred to and identified as the separate property of one of the Trustors. For this agreement and the presumption to be operable, no recordation during the lifetimes of either or both Trustors of a deed or other instrument terminating the joint tenancy and transferring title to a community property form of ownership or to the trust shall be required provided that the conveyancing instrument is in a form ready for recordation or is otherwise acceptable to third parties, including but not limited to transfer agents, title insurance and escrow companies.

Trying to read 35 or so pages of this kind of writing causes the trustors and their successor trustees NOT TO READ the documents that they are paying for so dearly. As a result, they tend to give up . . . and hope for the best.

Is there a better way than the intent paragraph above? We think so. A concise "Declaration of Intent" paragraph should immediately follow the preamble declaration.

Such an intent paragraph might read as—

The purpose of this Trust and the intent of its Trustors is to provide for the protection and management of the Trustors' assets during their lifetimes, and to provide for the orderly disposition of said assets upon the death of the Trustors, without supervision by any Court. Upon the death of the surviving Trustor, the successor beneficiaries of this trust shall be the Trustors' children, grandchildren, and others as designated, who are alive at the time of such death.

For sequence purposes, we would designate the above paragraph or any of its variants as **Article 1**.

The clause "without supervision by any Court" (cited above) presupposes an inter vivos trust whereby most of the intended trust property is retitled in the name of the family trust. This predeath arrangement is the classic step for avoiding probate when one or both trustors die.

Article 2: Termination Events

Traditionally, professional trust preparers, especially those associated with law and CPA firms, bank and insurance trust departments, and other corporate trustees, want to keep a trust with substantial assets active as long as possible. One way they do this is to conceal the events which terminate the trust in the bottom one-third of the trust agreement. Another way they keep a trust alive, when it otherwise could be terminated, is by endless legal proceedings in the probate court having jurisdiction over the trust property. In this manner, legal and professional fees draw down the trust assets disturbingly fast.

Unlike a family corporation which has indefinite life, all family trusts must terminate. The events causing termination are established by the trustors, and executed when appropriate by successor trustees down the family line. The problem is: the events are seldom clearly specified in layman terms.

Example objective termination events are:

1. When the youngest living beneficiary attains a specified age: 25, 30, 35 . . . or whatever.

2. Upon informed consent of the majority of beneficiaries who see no particular benefit to themselves in continuing the trust, beyond an orderly windup and closure.

3. Frequent and substantial invasions of the trust corpus (principal) for emergencies and care of a "special needs" beneficiary. The trust itself may continue for this one beneficiary, and be terminated for all others.

4. Ongoing disputes by cantankerous beneficiaries who are never satisfied with their share of the income and principal. When threatened with legal proceedings by such a beneficiary, see the proceedings through, then terminate the trust for that person.

5. Establishing a "years certain" time limit for administration of the trust: 10, 20, 30 . . . or whatever.

6. When trust administration becomes "uneconomical." The commonly accepted threshold for this is $100,000 but can be set much higher for high-value trusts.

The above listing of events is intended to be instructive only. Our point is that, whatever termination events are established by the trustors, the events should be set forth up front in the trust instrument. We suggest this being **Article 2**, for example.

Designation of Successor Trustees

Our position is that only family members or close relatives should be designated as successor trustees to the creators of a family trust. While such persons may not be expert in trust administration, they can always engage professional assistance, if needed.

A family member trustee should be reasonably mature, and have accounting integrity, composure with beneficiaries, and ability to get things done. Once the trust is funded and operational, most activities will be income tax oriented. The Form 1041 preparation and its filing are once a year. Otherwise, ordinary checkbook accounting and property management monthly are required.

We object to any attorney, whether a family member or not, being a successor trustee or even a co-trustee. Attorneys are necessary for legal advocacy purposes. Generally, they are not good administrators. By nature and training they intimidate and attack the credibility of everyone except themselves. Keep them out of any trustee role in your trust affairs. The same applies to corporate trustees (who are attorneys) in the trust department of banks, insurance companies, and other financial institutions.

Comb through your trust instrument in search for what we call the "slip-in of co-trustee" clause, or the clause addressing "vacancy of trusteeship." To illustrate what we mean, we cite the following two examples extracted from professionally prepared trust instruments.

Example 1: Co-trustee slip-in—

Upon the death, inability to serve, or resignation of the husband **or wife** [trustors], the other of the two shall serve as sole trustee, with the power, however, to appoint **any other person** [attorney?] **or bank** as co-trustee. Upon the death, inability to serve, or resignation of **both** husband and wife [trustors], the successor trustee **shall be** such person or bank as is then serving as co-trustee. [Emphasis added.]

Example 2: Vacancy in trusteeship—

In the event a vacancy in the Trusteeship occurs and there are no Trustors or legally competent beneficiaries surviving, the court having jurisdiction over the Trust may appoint a successor trustee [of its choosing].

A court will always appoint an attorney as the successor trustee. It will especially do so in those situation where the trustors have been inattentive or procrastinative on such matters. Courts interpret every silence in a contractual document as acceptance of their appointees.

There is one antidote to a slip-in co-trustee or to a court-appointed successor trustee. The trustors MUST INSIST that their own family appointees be conspicuously named in the early portion of the trust agreement. Each family person could be designated sequentially as—

Successor Trustee #1 — full name
Successor Trustee #2 — full name
Successor Trustee #3 — full name
. . . or the survivor thereof.

Our "Example 1" above was found on page 20 of a 23-page trust instrument. "Example 2" was found on page 29 of a 37-page trust instrument. Because of the importance of trusteeship to a trust, we believe that listing of successor family trustees should appear no later than on page 2, and possible designated as **Article 3.**

Diagram of Intended Subtrusts

Those family trusts created by husband and wife usually have several pages of instructions captioned: *Division of Trust after Death of a Trustor* . . . or wording to this effect. Sample extracted wording goes like this—

The first trustor to die shall be called the "Deceased Trustor" and the living trustor shall be called the "Surviving Trustor." On the death of the Deceased Trustor, the Trustee shall divide the Trust Estate, including any additions to the Trust made from the decedent's Will, or by life insurance policies on the decedent's life, into three separate Trusts, designated as the "Survivor's Trust," the "Marital Trust," and the "Residual Trust."

The above instruction is followed by about four pages describing the subtrusts. Another four pages describe the subtrust distributions of income (and principal, when necessary) to the surviving trustor. Then, another three to four pages follow, captioned as: *Reformation of Trust after Death of Surviving Trustor* . . . or words to this effect.

The whole idea of the 10 to 12 pages is that the trust instrument is to arrange the subtrusts to parallel the major steps in the Form 706 accounting of the deceased trustor's property. The subtrusts also simplify the Form 1041 accounting of the deceased trustor's income while the surviving trustor is alive. The "survivor's trust" is nothing more than a Form 1040 accounting of income from the survivor's own property (before death). When the surviving trustor dies, Form 706 is required for the survivor's "reformed estate" (own property plus marital deduction property). Then all subtrusts plus the survivor's estate are reformed into one single trust for subsequent family trust administration.

We think that all of the 10 to 12 pages above can be formulated into one self-explanatory diagram. An example of such a diagram is presented in Figure 8.3.

There is no prohibition against including an instructive diagram in a family trust instrument. But have **you** ever seen any such diagram in a trust document? Have you ever talked to your trust preparer about including such a diagram? Which would you prefer: Reading 10 to 12 pages of attorney text or glancing at, then later studying, a diagram along the lines of Figure 8.3?

Preamble wording to the subtrust diagram could read as follows:

During their joint lifetimes, the Trustors shall be the sole and exclusive beneficiaries of this Trust. Upon the death of one of the Trustors, the Surviving Trustor shall be the sole and exclusive beneficiary of the Survivor's Trust, and shall be the sole lifetime beneficiary of the deceased Trustor's three subtrusts, as depicted in the accompanying diagram. Upon the death of the Surviving Trustor, all subtrusts plus the survivor's estate (including residual property in the Marital Trust) shall

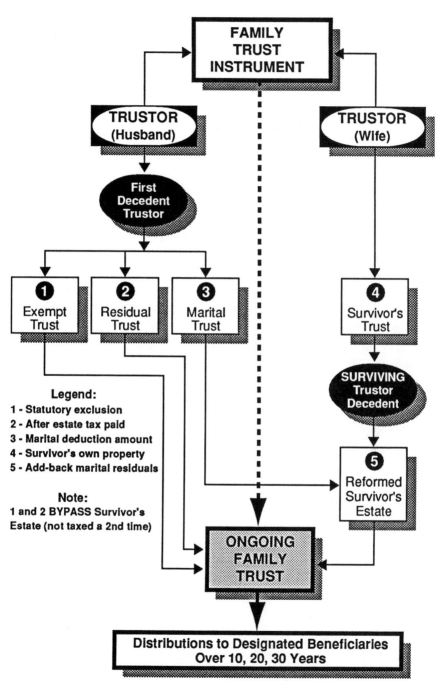

Fig. 8.3 - Diagram of Subtrust Arrangement After Each Trustor Dies

be reformed into a single Family Trust (also as depicted in the accompanying diagram). Once all expenses and taxes are paid, the Family Trust shall be administered by the Successor Trustee, as heretofore provided.

Could such wording (or its variant) and its "accompanying diagram" be designated as **Article 4**?

Beneficiary Prioritizing

Once the surviving trustor has deceased, the income and principal — ALL OF IT, eventually — are to be distributed. This is to be done at least no less frequently than once annually. Intelligent distribution rests on prioritizing the needs of the beneficiaries in an attempt to "level the economic field" in a reasonable manner.

The first step in this regard is to empower the successor trustee with broad discretion to make inquiry into the true needs of each recipient. For example, a beneficiary who is financially well off, having no serious medical problems, comfortable in his own home, has less distributive need than one who is struggling to make ends meet (with several children, one or more of college age).

The first order of prioritizing is to organize the trust or designated beneficiaries into what we call: "Tier levels." For example, said levels could be—

Tier 1 — Children, siblings, and parents of the trustors.

Tier 2 — Spouses of the children and siblings, grandchildren, and grand nephews/nieces.

Tier 3 — Other beneficiaries, including dear friends of the trustors and favored educational and charitable institutions.

Depending on the number of beneficiaries in each tier level, a maximum and minimum distribution range could be indicated. For example, Tier 1 could be set at 70% maximum and 50% minimum; Tier 2 at 30% maximum and 20% minimum; and Tier 3 at 20% maximum and 10% minimum. Possible combinations would be:

T/1 at 70% + T/2 at 20% + T/3 at 10% = 100%
T/1 at 60% + T/2 at 30% + T/3 at 10% = 100%
T/1 at 50% + T/2 at 30% + T/3 at 20% = 100%

For our purposes, the term "distribution" means *all of* the trust-generated income for a given year *plus* capital makeups from the trust principal (as needed). There should be no requirement that the principal be preserved to the very end. Except for an ongoing family business that is part of the trust property, a time-in-years trust termination could be set. We believe that no more than 30 years after the death of the surviving trustor would be a reasonable termination target (if other events did not shorten this time frame). Family trusts that go on and on for generations encourage fee milking by professionals, foster excessive administration expenses, and promote devastating litigative disputes.

If the above makes sense to you, it could be incorporated into your trust instrument as **Article 5**: *Distribution of Income and Principal to Beneficiaries*. Again, we yield to your trust preparer for the best wording to accomplish the ends sought.

Trust Property: Appendix A

In our proposed Article 1 above, there was a clause cited as: *without supervision of any court.* This means that the ultimate focus of administration of the family trust is the nature, extent, and value of the property therein. To the extent that property — such as real property, family business interests, the investment portfolio, etc. — are already in the trust, ownershipwise, no court probate is required. But what happens to those property items intended for the trust, if they are not in the trust when the surviving trustor dies?

Answer: *Technically*, there would be a probative estate to the extent of all residual property not already owned by the trust. However, a more practical view can be taken.

If more than 50% of the intended property is already owned by the trust when the surviving trustor dies, the survivor's executor can convey the residual property to it . . . without probate! This is the significance of the clause cited in Article 4 above: *including any additions to the Trust made from the decedent's Will* (bottom of page 8-13). Such "additions" should be made within six months of each trustor's death: the alternate valuation date.

The idea would be that after all debts, all death taxes, and all income taxes for each decedent trustor's estate have been paid, and all will-directed distributions of property have been made, the "rest and residue" shall be conveyed to the family trust. The document for recording the conveyances should be an **Appendix A**, "incorporated herein by reference." We yield to your trust preparer for the actual wording to be used.

Meanwhile, Appendix A could be titled: *Property of the Jones Family 2002 Trust*, for example. We would expect this appendix to be arranged into three separate time groupings, such as—

X — Initial property conveyed by the Joint Trustors;
Y — Subsequent property conveyed by the Surviving Trustor;
Z — Subsequent property reformed by the Successor Trustee.

For each subpart X, Y, and Z of Appendix A, each item of property conveyed should be accompanied by an appropriate recordation. The recordation should provide a description of the property, its market value, its date of conveyance, and a copy of its Grant Deed (for real property), authenticated ownership (of a business), and a statement of account (for portfolio items).

Incidentally, the value of property conveyed into trust may change between the date of death of a trustor and the settlement of the trustor's estate. If the time lapse between these two dates is more than nine months (the normal due date after death for filing Form 706), the property should be reappraised by an independent professional. Recall that the date of settlement of an estate is that date stamped on the IRS's Form 706 acceptance letter. Should the value of the property change between the time of filing Form 706 and its IRS acceptance, the successor trustee will need independent documentation of such fact.

Standard Clauses: Appendix B

We have previously indicated that a "typical" family trust instrument runs approximately 35 pages (excluding Appendix A).

Fully 25 of these 35 pages constitute what we refer to as: *standard clauses and powers*. They appear in every trust instrument as general terms and conditions which authenticate the trust. Such matters are NOT BENEFICIARY SPECIFIC.

Look through any family trust instrument that is available to you. Or, look through your own trust instrument which you have had prepared. Do you find any of the following-type clauses that specifically address the needs of your beneficiaries? The types of matters we are referring to are:

1. State court jurisdiction in event of disputes.
2. Compensation of trustee and "hold harmless" aspects.
3. Notification to trustee of events affecting distribution.
4. Spendthrift clauses against pledging trust assets.
5. Payments to minors and those under disability.
6. Payments to creditors and trust advisors.
7. Bank accounts and expense recordkeeping.
8. Right of residential occupancy of real property.
9. Provisions relating to life and health insurance.

Our position is that these types of clauses, and others similar, can be collated into one self-explanatory document of its own. Such a document could be designated as **Appendix B**: *Standard Clauses*. Introductory wording in the trust instrument could call attention to such an appendix ("incorporated by reference") but otherwise would be omitted from the primary focus of the trust arrangement.

Powers of Administration: Appendix C

By far, the bulk of any trust instrument is a complete recitation of the legal powers and duties of the trustee for administering the trust. Well over 90% of the cited powers are lifted directly from the Probate Code of the state having jurisdiction over the trust property. We don't understand why it is necessary to recite them in the trust when an **Appendix C**: *Powers of Administration*, would serve the trustee better.

The introductory wording to Appendix C could read as follows:

To carry out the provision of the Trust created by this instrument, the Trustee shall have the following powers in addition to those powers now or hereafter conferred by law:

1. *Power to Retain Trust Property*
2. *Power to Manage Trust Property*
3. *Power to Invest and Reinvest Trust Assets*
4. *Power to Borrow and Encumber Trust Assets*
5. *Power to Participate in Reorganizations and Liquidations*
6. *Power to Vote Securities*
7. *Power to Pay Taxes Assessed Against the Trust*
8. *Power to Hold Undivided Interests*
9. *Power to Initiate Litigation or Settle Claims*
10. *Power to Lease*
11. *Power to Lend Money to Trustors' Probate Estates*
12. *Power to Employ Agents and Delegates*
13. *Power to Insure Trust Assets Against Loss*
14. *Power to Register Securities in Nominee Name*
15. *Power to Administer Assets Without Physical Division*
16. *Power to Distribute in Kind*
17. *Power to Withhold Payment*
18. *Power to Release Powers*

Putting all of the above in perspective, we do not see the need for more than 10 pages of person-specific instructions in any family trust arrangement. (Extended family businesses and generation-skipping trusts may be exceptions.) Especially if there are only five Articles with Appendices A, B, and C each presented as a self-explanatory document on its own. Yes, of course, we realize that many trust preparers do not share our views.

Being only 10 pages (or less) instead of 35 (or more), each trustor is more likely to read and comprehend that which he and she are paying for. To verify such reading, each trustor can be asked to initial and date each such page in its lower right-hand corner.

9

GENERATION-SKIPPING TRUSTS

A "Skip Person" Is A Natural Person 2 Or More Generations Below The Generation Assignment Of The Transferor. Property Interests Transferred To Such Persons Are Subject To A SEPARATE 55% Tax, After Allocation Of A $1,000,000 (Inflation Indexed) Exemption Allowance. The Taxable Amount For Each Skip Person Is His/Her INCLUSION RATIO Times The Value Of The Property Transferred. The Tax Is Computed And Paid At Times Of: (1) Direct Skips, (2) Partial Distributions, And (3) Final Distributions. All Such Property Interests Must Vest Or Terminate Within 90 Years Of Creating A GST Trust.

When an individual transfers property gratuitously, either during life by gift or upon death by will or trust, a transfer tax applies. We covered this matter in Chapter 2: Imposition of Transfer Tax. We also mentioned that there was a GST tax imposed on generation-skipping transfers. Other than its introductory aspects, we did not dwell on the GST tax in Chapter 2; we want to do so now.

Ordinarily, when property is transferred through a family trust from one generation of individuals to the next generation, and from that generation to its next generation, there are two transfer tax impositions. There is an imposition when generation 0 transfers to generation 1, and again when there is a transfer from generation 1 to generation 2. By skipping over generation 1 and transferring directly to generation 2, one of the ordinarily two transfer taxes is avoided. The skipping over is perfectly legal, so long as the trustor's — the generation 0's — intent is expressly stated in the governing trust instrument. The only catch is: there is a tax imposed for the privilege of skipping over a generation.

For example, suppose $3,000,000 is transferred from generation 0 to generation 1. The transfer tax would be $1,650,000 (3,000,000 x 55%). If there were no skipovers, the transfer tax on the same $3,000,000 from generation 1 to generation 2 would also be $1,650,000. Thus, without skipovers, two successive generation transfers would produce a combined tax of $3,300,000. Stated another way, if skipovers were allowed without the imposition of a transfer tax, the U.S. Treasury would stand to lose $1,650,000 in revenue. With the GST tax and the GST exemption of $1,000,000, the Treasury loss is $550,000 (1,000,000 x 55%) instead of $1,650,000. Furthermore, this amount of loss is fixed no matter how many generational skipovers are involved.

In this chapter, therefore, we want to address the tax law on generation-skipping transfers, who is responsible for the tax (and when) and what some of the features are that make a GST trust different from that of an ordinary family trust. Such features include the "generation assignment" of heirs, the designation of "skip persons" for receiving corpus property, and the "allocation" of the $1,000,000 GST exemption among the skip persons. We may get a little technical when discussing such matters as "inclusion ratio," "deemed allocated," taxable distributions, and taxable terminations. We certainly want you to be aware of the 90-year antiperpetuity rule affecting all family trusts.

Overview of GST Law

Prior to 1976, there was no GST tax whatsoever. This meant that wealthy families could skip multiple generational lines, pass property to each of them, and pay only one transfer tax on the trust arrangement. This practice perpetuated wealth in those families who were financially fortunate. This open-ended practice was tempered somewhat on October 4, 1976 when the Tax Reform Act of that year [P.L. 94-455] went into effect.

In 1976, a GST tax was imposed on every grandchild of a transferor who gratuitously received in excess of $2,000,000. In

1986 (Tax Reform Act: P.L. 99-514), the 1976 law was repealed. It was replaced with a single $1,000,000 exemption for all grandchildren combined, down all generational lines. The 1986 Act is effective for all GST trusts created or reformed after October 22, 1986. For those trusts created earlier, there are transitional rules and grandfathered clauses that permit some of the 1976 rules to apply. Hence, for our purposes we will address only the GST trusts created after October 22, 1986.

The 1986 law codified all GST matters as Chapter 13 of the Internal Revenue Code. This IRC chapter is titled: *Tax on Generation-Skipping Transfers*. Chapter 13 consists of the following subchapters:

A — Tax Imposed
B — Generation-Skipping Transfers
C — Taxable Amount
D — GST Exemption
E — Applicable Rate; Inclusion Ratio
F — Other Definitions and Special Rules
G — Administration

All total, IRC Chapter 13 consists of 26 separate tax law sections: 2601 (*Tax Imposed*) through 2663 (*Regulations*). Section 2601 reads in full as—

A tax is hereby imposed on every generation-skipping transfer (within the meaning of subchapter B [Estate and Gift Taxes]*).*

The Chapter 13 above mentioned is "within . . . subchapter B." The GST tax is IN ADDITION TO the gift and death transfer taxes that have been previously discussed.

Fundamental Definitions

Already we have used the letters "GST" several times. The "GS", of course, stands for: Generation-Skipping. It is the "T" that often causes misunderstanding. The "T" stands for: Transfer(s). It does not stand for "tax," nor does it stand for "trust." The "T" is for the transfer of property from a transferor (donor, grantor, trustor) to a transferee (recipient, distributee, or beneficiary).

With these GST letters now clarified, we ask: What are the fundamental aspects of GST activities that give you a "quick handle" on what GST trusts are all about?

Answer: You need to know the definitions of a skip person and a non-skip person, and how generation assignments are made.

First: Who is a "skip person"? The whole concept of the GST tax is premised upon there being one or more skip persons in the family hierarchy. Section 2613(a) defines such a person as—

(1)   a natural person assigned to a generation which is 2 or more generations below the generation assignment of the transferor, OR

(2)   a trust . . . if all [property] *interests in such trust are held by skip persons . . . and at no time after such transfer* [into trust] *may a distribution . . . be made from such trust to a non-skip person.*

A non-skip person is any person who is not a skip person.

Hence, for an arrangement to qualify as a GST trust, the property/corpus transfers from the trustor must ultimately go to all skip persons. Non-skip persons may be included in the trust instrument, but only to the extent that they are *income* recipients: not corpus recipients. It is important, therefore, that the trust instrument make the distinction clear as to which beneficiaries are skip persons and which are non-skip persons.

Under ordinary familial conditions, a GST trust would provide for non-skip persons as well as for its skip persons. Because non-skip persons receive no corpus from the trust, they get priority on all of its income. A non-skip person may disclaim all of his/her income share or may decline part of it. In such case, the disclaimed/declined income would go to other non-skip persons (or to skip persons) having the most financial need. So important is this separation of distribution rights between non-skip and skip persons that we present a depiction of the process in Figure 9.1. If you grasp this one fundamental concept alone, you have taken a long step towards understanding the workings of a GST trust.

Fig. 9.1 - Distribution Distinction Between Non-Skip and Skip Persons

Generation Assignments?

What if the GST trust instrument does not make clear which beneficiaries are skip persons and which are non-skip? The only clear statement is that the trustor intends to make corpus distributions to his grandchildren and others downline. In this situation, the trustor — and ultimately the trustee — must follow the rules of Section 2651: *Generation Assignment.* This is a 1,000-word tax law with special subrules of its own.

The substance of Section 2651 is that there are three groupings of generation assignments. These are:

1. Lineal descendants, starting with the grandparent of the transferor [Sec. 2651(b)].

2. Marital descendants, starting with the marriage of any lineal descendant [Sec. 2651(c)].

3. Nonlineal descendants, starting with those persons born not more than $12^{1}/2$ years after birth of the transferor, and repeating every 25 years thereafter [Sec. 2651(d)].

A diagram of these assignment groupings is presented in Figure 9.2. Note that a "parent" is the *transferor reference* for starting the 25-year generational clock. A transferor and his or her spouse (or

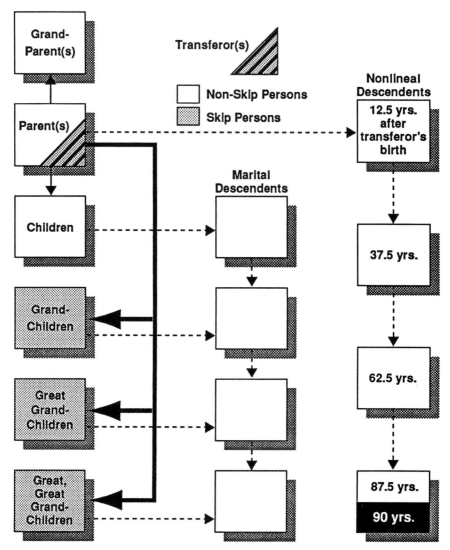

Fig. 9.2 - Depiction of Generational Groupings for GST Purposes

former spouse) share the same generation assignment. Similarly, a transferee and his or her spouse share the same generation assignment.

Note in Figure 9.2 that a parent transferor is preceded by a grandparent. As per subsection 2651(b)(1), a grandparent is the starting person for the lineal descendancy assignments. This makes sense in that the generational groupings above the transferor, on par with the transferor, and below the transferor are all non-skip persons. Because GSTs are formed by families of wealth, the non-skips (presumably) would not want their estates to be further tax burdened with property transfers they do not need.

For persons who are not lineal descendants (siblings, nephews, nieces, cousins — called: "collateral heirs"), Section 2651(d) applies. This rule references the date of birth of the transferor and uses a 25-year band (12$^{1}/2$ years before and 12$^{1}/2$ years after) for establishing a new generation every 25 years. Such is our portrayal in Figure 9.2.

All of the above is fine, if all lineal descendants are alive when the corpus property is to be transferred. But, what happens if a parent in the lineal chain is deceased at the time of transfer? In this situation, Section 2651(e): *Special Rule for Persons with a Deceased Parent*, applies. The substance of this rule is that, if a parent (and his or her spouse) are deceased within 90 days of any GST transfer, all generation assignments "move up" one generation. This moving up would have the effect of converting a grandchild, who normally would be the first skip person generation, from a skip person to a non-skip person. This "predeceased parent" rule, as it is called, applies to all GS transfers after December 31, 1997.

Other Key Definitions

We are not through yet with fundamental definitions affecting GST matters. You need to know the significance of such terms as: direct skips, taxable distributions, and taxable terminations. These and related matters are addressed in IRC Section 2612: *Taxable Termination*; *Taxable Distribution*; *Direct Skip*. This is a 500-word tax law. It is supported by 2,500 words of regulatory text, namely: Regulation § 26.2612-1: *Definitions*.

A *direct skip* is the transfer of property (corpus or principal) directly to a skip person by a transferor who is subject to the regular gift/death transfer tax. Only one direct skip occurs when a single transfer of property skips two or more generations. A direct skip assignment usually takes place at the time the regular transfer tax is computed. As a consequence, the GST tax is added onto the regular transfer tax computed on Form 706. It is paid by the transferor out of his or her estate [Sec. 2623].

A *taxable distribution* is the distribution of corpus property from a GST trust to a skip person. The property transfer is "taxable" in the sense that the GST tax has not been previously paid. In this case, the GST tax is paid by the distributee out of his/her share of the transferred property. Hence, the transferee/distributee actually receives less property than otherwise, by the amount of GST taxes and expenses incurred [Sec. 2621].

A *taxable termination* is a termination (for any reason) of a property interest in the GST trust by a skip person. In other words, once a skip person has received, disclaimed, or abandoned his designated GST property, he is no longer a skip person for generation assignment purposes. If he thereafter receives income from the trust, which he may, he is treated as a non-skip person. When a termination of property transfers occurs, the trustee pays GST tax and expenses, and subtracts said amount from the property interests being terminated [Sec. 2622].

As per Section 2624: ***Valuation***, if property is transferred to a skip person as a result of the death of a transferor, its value for GST purposes is its value for estate tax purposes. This provides the benefit of an "estate freeze" in the initial property valuations, even though distributions and terminations may be made many years after the transferor's death. Otherwise, transfers during life are property valued at the time of the generation-skipping transfer.

For more effective assignment of GST property, it is better to designate property to grandchildren, great-grandchildren, etc. only after a transferor's death. At this time, more will be known about the financial needs of non-skip persons. A GST trustor/transferor can too easily get carried away with skip person transfers. The result could be the deprivation of an accustomed lifestyle by some less fortunate non-skip person in the family.

GST Exemption Amount

Probably the most attractive feature of a GST trust is its $1,000,000 exemption before the GST tax applies. This is a *per individual transferor/trustor* exemption. (It is NOT a per skip person exemption.) It is separate and apart from, and is in addition to, the unified gift/death exemption amount previously discussed in Chapter 2: Imposition of Transfer Tax. For an estate over $3,000,000, a $1,000,000 exemption nets the skip persons another $550,000 in property values. This is because the GST tax rate is a flat 55% of the skip person's property values at time of transfer.

The tax law on point is Section 2631(a): *GST Exemption*; *General Rule*. This section reads in most part as—

Every individual shall be allowed an exemption of $1,000,000 which may be allocated by such individual (or his executor) to any property with respect to which such individual is the transferor. [Emphasis added.]

In other words, for married individuals who are transferors/ trustors, there are *two separate* $1,000,000 exemptions. There is no joint exemption, and there is no interspousal transferability of the unused portion of either spouse's exemption. This prohibition alone creates an incentive for each transferor to allocate his or her entire exemption amount. One trustor could allocate to one set of grandchildren; the other trustor to another set. Better yet, formulate a joint skip person *exempt subtrust* (a "trust" as per Sec. 2613(a)(2)) with earmarked property interests totaling $2,000,000.

For generation-skipping transfers taking place after 1998, the $1,000,000 amount is indexed for inflation [Sec. 2631(c)]. Each year, there is a cost-of-living adjustment in $10,000 increments. If an annual adjustment does not equal or exceed a multiple of $10,000, the increase in the exemption amount is rounded to the next lowest multiple of $10,000. For example, if the inflation adjustment were 0.035 (which is 3$1/2$%), the tentative adjustment amount would be $35,000 ($1,000,000 x 0.035). The allowable exemption amount for that year would be $10,030,000 (which is 3 multiples of $10,000 each). Thus, while a transferor is alive, the annual inflation adjustments could have a significant impact on his allocating the cumulatively adjusted exemption amount to selected skip persons. This could include an exempt GST subtrust.

Self-Allocation or Deemed?

In the citation of Section 2631(a) above, we emphasized the phrase: *which may be allocated . . .* by such individual (or his executor). Whenever there is a "may" in a tax law, it means that one has the option of doing something or doing nothing. The "doing something" means that you call the shots. The "doing nothing" means that the IRS calls the shots. The doing something means self-allocating the GST $1,000,000+ exemption among the skip persons of your choice.

Doing something also means that Section 2632(a): *Time and Manner of Allocation*, comes into play. This section picks up the "which may be allocated" theme as follows:

> *Any allocation by an individual of his GST exemption under section 2631(a) may be made at any time on or before the date prescribed for filing the estate tax return for such individual's estate (determined with regard to extensions).*

What the "may be made at any time" means is while alive on Form 709 (Gift Tax Return) or upon death on Form 706 (Estate Tax Return). The latest due date for doing so is generally nine months after the transferor/trustor dies. A six-month's extension of this regular due date, however, can be requested and authorized.

If no self-allocation is made, the *deemed allocation* rules of Sections 2632(b) and (c) take over. The order of deemed allocation is such that the $1,000,000+ exemption is consumed very early in the property transferring process. The sooner it is consumed, the better it is for the IRS: less tracking time and more revenue.

For example, suppose the GST exemption amount, inflation adjusted, is $1,200,000. The transferor has three grandchildren ages 30, 20, and 10. He intends to transfer to each of them $2,000,000 when they reach age 35. He has the choice of spreading the $1,200,000 exemption equally among them ($400,000 per grandchild) or assigning the entire amount to the youngest grandchild. If he leaves it up to the IRS, the entire exemption will be "deemed allocated" to the oldest grandchild. Here, it will be immediately consumed, leaving no exemption allocation for the two younger grandchildren.

As we summarize in Figure 9.3, the choice is yours.

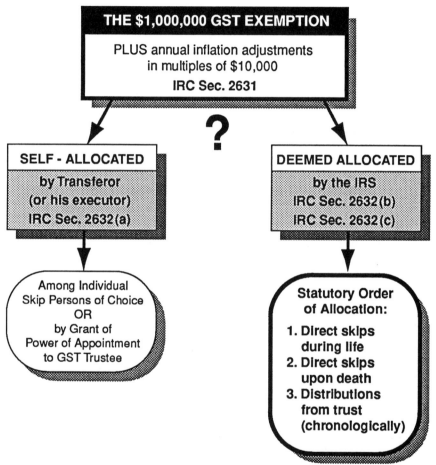

Fig. 9.3 - Allocating the $1,000,000 GST Exemption: Self or Deemed?

Why is self-allocation so important? Answer: Differences in appreciation potential of the exempt property.

In the example above, there are 25 years of appreciation potential before the 10-year-old grandchild reaches age 35. The $1,200,000 allocated exemption amount of property might easily reach $5,000,000 by then. If it does, the entire $5,000,000 is GST tax exempt. We think this makes a strong case for self-allocation upon death, rather than during life.

How Allocations Made

Section 2632(a)(2): *Manner* (of allocation) says—

The [IRS] *shall prescribe by forms or regulations the manner in which any allocation* [of the GST exemption] *is to be made.*

We prefer to acquaint you with the forms required rather than with the regulations. Accordingly, the pertinent forms are:

Form 706 (Sch. R) — Generation-Skipping Transfer Tax
   • Part 1 — GST Exemption Reconciliation
   • Part 2 — Direct Skips Bearing the GST Tax
   • Part 3 — Direct Skips Not Bearing the GST Tax
   • Sch. R-1 — GST Tax on Direct Skips from a [pre-existing] Trust [for the decedent]

As you may recall, Form 706 is fully titled: *U.S. Estate (and Generation-Skipping Transfer) Tax Return*. This form requires the listing and valuation of all property interests of the decedent at time of death. Before any of these property interests can be allocated to the GST "exemption bank," all property interests intended for skip persons must be listed, as applicable, on Schedules A through I of Form 706. These asset schedules are titled, respectively—

Sch. A — Real Estate
Sch. B — Stocks & Bonds
Sch. C — Mortgages, Notes, & Cash
Sch. D — Insurance on Decedent's Life
Sch. E — Jointly Owned Property
Sch. F — Other Miscellaneous Property
Sch. G — Transfers During Decedent's Life
Sch. H — Powers of Appointment
Sch. I — Annuities

The property values entered on these schedules, when accepted by the IRS, become the *estate values* for allocating the GST exemption.

Part 1 of Schedule R: Exemption Reconciliation, summarizes the allocations as—

1. *Maximum allowable GST exemption*   _____

2. *Total GST exemption allocated to intervivos transfers and direct skips* [from estates]   _____

3. *GST exemption available to allocate to trusts* (subtract item 2 from item 1)   _____

Why not minimize summary 2 and maximize summary 3? If so, the downstream trust inclusion ratio would be reduced.

Inclusion Ratio for GST Trusts

The official caption of summary 3 is: *Allocation of GST exemption to trusts (as defined for GST tax purposes).* What is this caption all about?

The short answer is: Unless the maximum allowable GST exemption is consumed on Schedule R for Form 706 purposes, the unused portion is available for those property transfers taking place years later. Because of the appreciation potential of the GST exemption-allocated property, mentioned earlier, we urge that the bulk of the maximum allowable exemption — even 100% of it — be "reserved" for non-Schedule R purposes.

We like to think of Schedule R (Form 706) as the *deemed allocation* mandates. Our strategy, depicted in Figure 9.4, is to compute and pay the GST tax at the time of future distributions and terminations, rather than at the time of Form 706 filing. There is, however, one complication and catch. It is the concept of an **inclusion ratio** with respect to the skip person property transfers.

The inclusion ratio is the fraction of property transferred to skip persons that is subject to the GST tax rate of 55%. The determination of this ratio or fraction is prescribed by Section 2642: *Inclusion Ratio Defined* (consisting of about 2,000 words) and by

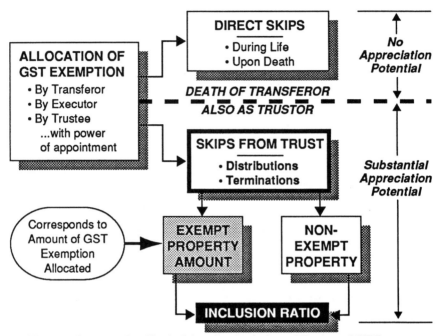

Fig. 9.4 - Strategy for Maximizing Appreciation of Exempt GST Property

Regulation § 26.2642-1(a): *Inclusion Ratio; General* (consisting of about 5,000 words).

In the most succinct terms possible, the *inclusion ratio* is 1 **minus** an "applicable fraction" of any generation-skipping transfer of property from a trust. Stated another way—

Inclusion ratio = 1 – applicable fraction

The applicable fraction (A/F), in turn, is—

$$A/F = \frac{\text{Allocated amount of GST exemption}}{\text{Estate Value of Property} - [\text{death tax} + \text{charitable deduction}]}$$
When Allocated

Obviously, the greater the amount of the maximum allowable GST exemption allocated to the trust, the larger the applicable fraction (for a given property transfer), and the *lower* the inclusion ratio. Bear in mind that the term "value of property" is the estate value (on Form 706) of the property transferred and not its current appreciated value.

The term "death tax" in our formula above is a combination of federal and state death taxes plus associated charges borne by the property interests designated for transfer. In other words, property transferred to skip persons has to bear its prorata share of all taxes, costs, and charitable deductions (if any) that all other property bears. Skip person transferees get no free ride on the backs of other transfers to non-skip persons.

How/When GST Tax Paid

The GST tax for direct skips is computed on Schedule R (Form 706) and is paid at the time Form 706 is filed. We covered this earlier. We have yet to address taxable distributions and taxable terminations. A glance at Figure 9.5 will give you an overview of the timing and importance of tax payment. When the GST tax is paid, the property interests vest fully in the skip person distributee.

A "taxable distribution" is the distribution of property from a trust to a skip person. The distribution(s) take place *after* Form 706 has been filed (with its GST tax on direct skips) and accepted by the IRS. These distributions are transfer taxable because they have not been previously GST taxed. How is this tax computed and paid?

It is computed by means of the following two IRS forms—

706-GS(D-1):   *Notification of Distribution from a Genera-tion-Skipping Trust* (prepared by trustee)

706-GS(D):   *Generation-Skipping Transfer Tax Return for Distributions* (prepared by distributee)

Form 706-GS(D-1) is prepared by the trustee for each skip person distributee. If there were three distributees for a given calendar year, there would be three Forms GS(D-1).

Each Form GS(D-1) describes the property distributed, its date of distribution, its inclusion ratio, and its value at time of distribution. The product of the inclusion ratio times the property value is the: *Amount of Transfer*. In this regard, it is important to

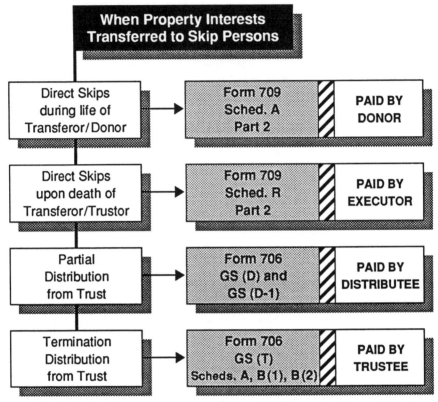

Fig. 9.5 - Tax Returns to prepare Before GST Property Interests Vest

be aware that the value of property designated for transfer (for GST **exemption** purposes) is its *estate value*. The estate value is used only for the purpose of computing the inclusion ratio. This way, the inclusion ratio is fixed for all actual subsequent transfers. At the time of an actual transfer, the current value of the property is used. Such value is what the skip person would actually receive.

Each skip person distributee uses Form GS(D-1) to prepare his own Form GS(D). Part III of the GS(D): *Tax Computation*, consists of 10 lines. The "start" line is: *Total transfers* which, recall, is each property's inclusion ratio times its current value. The "end" line is: *Net GST tax*. This tax is **paid by the distributee**. Form 706-GS(D) is a separate return of its own and is filed—

No later than April 15 of the year following the calendar year when the distributions were made.

A "taxable termination" is the final distribution of a skip person's property interests. A termination distribution is usually made upon a skip person reaching a trustor designated age (25, 30, 35) or earlier upon such person's death. The "termination" ends that distributee's property interests, but not the trust itself.

The GST tax on termination distributions is computed on Form 706-GS(T): *Generation-Skipping Transfer Tax Return for Terminations.* This is a 3-page form prepared by the trustee on a calendar year basis. It summarizes all termination distributions for the year and assigns to each distributee's property interests a prorata burden of the trust's debts, expenses, and taxes (other than the GST tax). The GST tax is **paid by the trustee.** Thereafter, each termination distributee receives his final property interests *minus*, of course, his prorata share of the GST tax.

Rule Against Perpetuities

Once a generation-skipping arrangement is established and its techniques mastered, the familial desire is to go on and on, ad infinitum. Perpetual family trusts are envisioned for transferring property interests down generational lines to unnamed and yet-to-be-born distributees. Such a goal contradicts the common-law rule against perpetuity which has been around since early times. The premise of common law is that if a property interest conveyed by trust does not vest in some life-in-being within 21 years after the death of an individual alive at the time the trust was created, the interest is invalid. Thereupon, the property escheats to the state having original jurisdiction over the trust. This escheat aspect has led to endless litigation over the certainty of the vesting period.

To establish more certainty in permissible vesting periods, the National Conference of Commissioners on Uniform State Laws made a study of perpetuity cases in litigation during the period 1984-89. The conference members (attorneys representing different states) found that the average age of the youngest life-in-being was six years old. Using the Bureau of Census statistics for life expectancies in 1986, a person six years old then would live, actuarially, 69 years. Adding the "plus 21 years" under common law, the conference members adopted 90 years (69 + 21) as a reasonable gestation time for property interests to vest. In 1990, the 90-year gestation period was recommended for enactment by all uniformity-minded states.

In 1991, California (as an example) enacted its own *Statutory Rule Against Perpetuities*: Sections 21205 through 21209 of its Probate Code (CPC). The CPC Section 21205: *Nonvested Property Interests*, reads—

A nonvested property interest is invalid unless one of the following conditions is satisfied:

    (a) When the interest is created, it is certain to vest or terminate no later than 21 years after the death of an individual then alive.

    (b) The interest either vests or terminates within 90 years after its creation.

Furthermore, CPC Section 21209: *Posthumous births*, reads in full—

In determining whether a nonvested property interest or a power of appointment is valid, the possibility that a child will be born to an individual after the individual's death is disregarded.

In 1992, the IRS adopted the 90-year vesting period for family trusts. It did so via its GST Regulation § 26.2601-1(b)(1)(v)(B)(2): *Special rule for certain powers of appointment.* We had this special (anti-perpetuity) rule in mind when we displayed in Figure 9.2 the box labeled "90 yrs" at the very end of the third column. Overall, therefore, we see no validity in a GST trust conveying property interests to more than three generations of skip persons.

10

SOURCES OF TRUST INCOME

> **Property In A Family Trust Should Preferably Be Of A Type Which Produces Current Income. Among Such Sources Are Taxable Interest, Tax-Exempt Interest, Ordinary Dividends (From Publicly-Held Corporations), Profits And Dividends From Family-Owned Corporations, Rents And Royalties From Real Estate (Including Farm Land) And Natural Resources, And Pooled Ownership In Partnerships, S Corporations, Other Trusts, and Mortgage Conduits. When Converting From One Form Of Property To Another, Or When Liquidating An Asset Altogether, Schedule D (Form 1040): CAPITAL GAINS And LOSSES Is Vital.**

One purpose of a family trust is to acquire and hold property which can produce income over an extended period of time. After expenses, deductions, etc., the net income is passed through to the trust beneficiaries for whatever use each sees fit. The foremost beneficiary in this regard is the surviving trustor. Being an older person . . . and getting older (65, 75, 85, 95), it is most important that such a person have the assurance of income for life. This is the purpose of the marital trust, QTIP trust, and QDOT trust that we described in Chapter 7.

As to beneficiaries other than the surviving trustor, the distribution of income from the trust can be thought of as an "opportunity leveler." The degree to which this leveling can be achieved depends on the extent of discretion empowered to the trustee by the trustor. As we discussed in the latter part of Chapter

8, there are three tiers of leveling effort. There is Tier 1: economic and comfort leveling; there is Tier 2: educational and medical leveling; and Tier 3: gratuitous and charitable leveling.

To facilitate the leveling discretion of the trustee, the sources of trust income must be reliable and continuous. The income must derive from legitimate investments and businesses, and from sound co-ownership arrangements. The trust, being a legal entity of its own, can be the owner or part-owner of any form of business or property holdings it desires. Furthermore, the income property acquired need not be held until the trust terminates. The trustee has the power to sell, exchange, or reacquire other property as he/she deems prudent.

In this chapter, therefore, we want to review all eligible sources of trust income, and discuss briefly the pros and cons of each. This includes reference to the tax schedules that support the income entries on Form 1041: *U.S. Income Tax Return for Estates and Trusts*. We'll concentrate exclusively on the trust entity, and will bypass the estate of any deceased trustor. Our presumption in this chapter is that both trustors are deceased and the trust property is being reformed into a long-term arrangement of conservative assets seeking both income and growth. Always keep in mind that the trustee is a property *manager* only. He/she is **not** an active entrepreneur in the day-to-day operations of whatever business or businesses underlie the assets being held in trust.

Sources Listed on Form 1041

Page 1 of Form 1041 lists eight types of legitimate income sources. All are combined to comprise the *Total Income* of the trust. After listed deductions and other adjustments, the result is *Distributable Net Income* (DNI). It is this DNI amount that is distributable to the designated beneficiaries of the trust.

The eight types of income are:

1. Interest income
2. Ordinary dividends
3. Business income or <loss>
4. Capital gain or <loss>

5. Rents, royalties, partnerships, etc.
6. Farm income or <loss>
7. Ordinary gain or <loss>
8. Other income: type and amount

Compare this listing, if you will, with those income sources preprinted on Form 1040: U.S. *Individual* Income Tax Return. On Form 1040, there are 15 types of income. Thus, there are seven (15 – 8) fewer recognized types on Form 1041 than on Form 1040. Why is this, do you suppose?

To answer our "why" question, we list below those seven income sources on Form 1040 which DO NOT APPEAR on Form 1041. These are:

a. Wages, salaries, tips, etc.
b. Refunds of state income taxes
c. Alimony received
d. IRA distributions
e. Pensions and annuities
f. Unemployment compensation
g. Social security benefits

If you analyze these Form 1040 income sources (and exclude item b), what feature do they have in common? Answer: They represent *personal service* income of one type or another.

As interpreted for Form 1041 purposes, there can be no personal service income assigned to the trust by a trustor, the trustee, or any beneficiary thereof. In other words, the income reportable on Form 1041 is of a passive and investment type rather than a personal service type. This clarifies the point that a family trust is an *income distribution entity* . . . only. It is not an opportunity to shelter personal service income by those who have a financial interest in the trust.

Interest & Dividend Income

The most passive of passive-type income for a trust is its interest and dividend income. Here we are addressing *taxable* interest and dividend income as opposed to tax-exempt interest and dividends. We will address the aspects of tax-exempt income later, as there is no entry line on Form 1041 for such purpose.

Also on Form 1041, no official tax schedule is prescribed for listing the sources of interest or dividend income as there is on Form 1040. At each of the lines *Taxable interest* and *Ordinary dividends* on Form 1040 there is an instruction which reads:

Attach Schedule B if required.

Schedule B: Interest and Dividends is a required attachment to Form 1040 if either the interest or dividends exceeds $400

Modest and above-modest family trusts deal with much larger amounts of capital — several to many millions of dollars — than that available for investment by ordinary individuals. Hence, we think it is prudent to attach Schedule B (Form 1040) to Form 1041 for the itemized listing of every taxable interest source and every ordinary dividend source the trust may have. Schedule B, Part 1, can accommodate **15** separate interest sources, whereas its Part 2 can accommodate **20** ordinary dividend sources. This is all good recordkeeping and accounting should some beneficiary or other person make accusations of trust management improprieties.

The Form 1041 instructions for taxable interest income list the following examples of such income:

- *Accounts with banks, credit unions, and thrifts.*
- *Certificates of deposit and money market accounts.*
- *Notes, loans, and mortgages.*
- *U.S. Treasury bills, notes, and bonds.*
- *U.S. savings bonds.*
- *Original issue discounts.*

The Form 1041 instructions for reporting ordinary dividends simply say—

Report the trust's share of all ordinary dividends received during the tax year. Report capital gain distributions on Schedule D (Form 1041).

The payers of the above income report the information to the IRS on Forms 1099-INT, 1099-OID, and 1099-DIV, as appropriate. As depicted in Figure 10.1, a diligent trustee will match every entry on Schedule B (1040) to its corresponding Form 1099. Each Form 1099, by the way, must carry the EIN of the trust. We discussed the importance of the trust EIN in Chapter 8

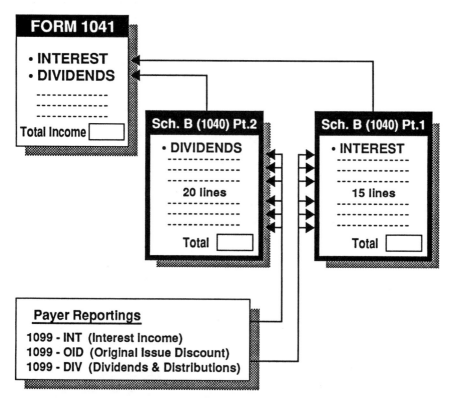

Fig. 10.1 - Documenting Interest & Dividend Income from Multiple Assets

Tax-Exempt Interest

On an individual Form 1040, there is an income entry line which reads—

Tax-exempt interest. DO NOT include on [Schedule B] ▶ $____

This line is a "side entry" only. It is not included in the aggregation of total income. The primary reason for showing it is to include it in a worksheet calculation that computes the portion of social security benefits that are taxed. There is no counterpart for social security taxation on Form 1041.

As a result, there is no corresponding income entry line for tax-exempt interest on Form 1041. So, how would one know that tax-exempt interest is indeed a legitimate income source for a trust?

Probably the most authentic way of knowing is to respond to Question 1 in the *Other Information* section on page 2 of Form 1041. That question reads—

Does the . . . trust receive tax-exempt income? ☐ *Yes,* ☐ *No. If "Yes," attach a computation of the allocation of expenses. Enter the amount of tax-exempt interest income and exempt-interest dividends* ▶ $_____.

The statutory authority for tax-exempt interest and exempt-interest dividends is IRC Section 103: *Interest on State and Local Bonds*. Subsection 103(a): *Exclusion*, reads—

Except as provided in subsection (b), gross income does not include interest on any state or local bond.

Subsection (b) carves out a taxable exception for private activity bonds, arbitrage bonds, and those not in registered form.

Except for the exceptions, if $100,000 of interest or dividend income was derived from exempt-qualified state and local bonds — called: *Municipal bonds* — it would be totally tax exempt. This means that $100,000 could be passed through to the beneficiaries of the trust, and none of them would pay any federal income tax on their share of the pass-through amount.

How could $100,000 of tax-exempt income be generated by a family trust? Answer: By investing $2,000,000 in a mutual fund of municipal bonds paying 5% annual interest ($2,000,000 x 0.05 = $100,000). Yes, the corresponding taxable yield might be 7% [0.05 ÷ (1 – tax rate)]. But all such income would be taxable. Given a choice, most beneficieraries would prefer tax-free income.

Restructure Proprietorship Income

In the preprinted listing of income sources on Form 1041, two are identically captioned with those on Form 1040. The two income sources are:

Form 1040	Form 1041
Business income or <loss> — *attach Schedule C*	*Business income or <loss>* — *attach Schedule C (Form 1040)*
Farm income or <loss> — *attach Schedule F*	*Farm income or <loss>* — *attach Schedule F (Form 1040)*

The heading on Schedule C (1040) is: ***Profit or Loss from Business***. Its first spatial entry is: *Name of proprietor* (plus that person's SSN). Likewise for Schedule F: ***Profit or Loss from Farming***. Schedule F's first spatial entry also is: *Name of proprietor* (plus SSN).

At the bottom of page 1 of Schedules C and F, there is a line which is captioned: ***Net profit or <loss>***. This caption is followed by the instruction: *If a profit, enter . . . on **Schedule SE*** [Self-Employment Tax]. Schedule SE computes the social security and medicare taxes for the owning proprietor. There is no provision on Form 1041 for entering net profit on Schedule SE.

A "proprietor" is a person who owns a business or farm in *sole proprietorship* form. A sole proprietorship, in turn, is a one-person operation which is neither a trust nor a corporation. On this basis, obviously, a trust cannot be a proprietorship. Then why are these two proprietorship income lines on Form 1041?

Form 1041, recall, is titled: U.S. Income Tax Return for ESTATES **and** Trusts. Thus, the form is used for estates . . . and, separately, for trusts. The inclusion of proprietorship Schedules C and F, we believe, is intended primarily for the estates of proprietors who have died. Schedule D (1041) and Form 4797 — presented later — can be used to rearrange a proprietorship for trust purposes.

During the 18 to 36 months for settling an estate, our position is that a proprietorship business or farm should be restructured and reformed. If of significant gross income (over $350,000, say) and of significant asset value (over $1,000,000, say), it could be reformed into a partnership, an S corporation, a C corporation, or an LLC. (An LLC can be a single-owner limited liability company, treated as an entity rather than a proprietorship.) Unless the proprietorship business or farm has substantial real estate holdings (with good appreciation potential), it is better to transfer it to a willing and conscientious family member, or sell it outright to an unrelated third party.

Family Corporation Stock

Families of wealth often hold major ownership interests in large (over $5,000,000) closely-held business enterprises. Here, the term "closely-held" means five or fewer founders owning more than 50% of the enterprise. In other words, the enterprise — most often in corporate form — is owned privately: not publicly. When this happens, special stock ownership rules apply. Such is the role of IRC Section 318: *Constructive Ownership of Stock.*

The general rule on point is subsection (a)(1): *Members of Family.* This subsection reads in part—

An individual shall be considered as owning the stock owned, directly or indirectly, by or for . . . his spouse . . . and his children, grandchildren, and parents.

For our purposes, the term "individual" applies to the trustor (now deceased) who was the founder or one of the five or fewer founders of the corporate enterprise. Even though the founder's spouse, children, and parents may hold ostensible shares in the business, the presumption is that said shares were gratuitously transferred to them by the founder. This presumption holds unless a particular family member can show that he or she contributed capital (bought shares) independently out of pocket.

Thus, when the founder/trustor of the family corporation dies, the trust becomes the sole stockholder of all family member interests therein. At this point, subsection 318(a)(2)(B): *Attribution from Trusts*, applies. This rule reads—

> *Stock owned, directly or indirectly, by or for a trust . . . shall be considered as owned by its beneficiaries in proportion to the **actuarial interest** of such beneficiaries in such trust.*

Actuarial interest? How is this determined for each beneficiary?

This is where the trustee, with professional assistance, has to resort to the use of actuarial tables that we discussed briefly in Chapter 6: Charitable Remainder Trusts.

As a source of income to the trust, the profits and dividends of a family corporation would likely be scrutinized more closely by the IRS than if the enterprise were publicly held. Consequently, it could be advisable to employ nonfamily members as chief operating managers of the corporation. This way, all profits and dividends can be assigned directly to the trust.

Rents & Royalties Income

Many trustors build their retirement and afterlife wealth through rental real estate. They do so because rental properties possess three choice ingredients, namely:

(1) Potential for appreciation over long periods of time.
(2) Income production through rents and royalties.
(3) Tax sheltering through mortgage interest deductions and depreciation allowances for buildings, structures, and equipment; depletion allowances for natural deposits and oil and gas.

The preferred property includes residential buildings, commercial structures, natural resources, and sharecropping farmland.

During life, most real estate owners mortgage their property to the hilt and maximize their depreciation allowance, so that the net income is negative (meaning loss). This provides tax sheltering to other positive income sources, such as wages and salaries. With property in trust, however, the tax sheltering motivation is diminished. More preferably, net *positive* income is sought. This means paying down, as much as is prudent, any existing mortgages. Subsequently, the positive income is passed through to the beneficiaries who pay tax at diluted rates.

Income produced from rental real estate is reported on Form 1041 via Schedule E (Form 1040), Part I. A digest of this schedule is presented in Figure 10.2. We have omitted the portions of the official schedule which address the at-risk and passive *loss* limitation rules. With net positive **income** from trust property, you can ignore the passive loss rules.

Sch. E (1040)	INCOME OR LOSS FROM RENTAL REAL ESTATE AND ROYALTIES					Part I	
Property Kind and Location				Continuation Schedules			
A B C			[1]	[2]	[3]		
INCOME	A	B	C	D,E,F	G,H,I	TOTALS	
Rents							
Royalties							
EXPENSES							
14 Items							
Depreciation							
Depletion							
TOTAL EXPENSES							
Income							
Loss							
				NET INCOME OR LOSS ➡			

Fig. 10.2 - Accommodation of Multiple Properties on Schedule E (1040), Part 1

Although Schedule E (1040), Part I, is formatted for three rental properties (A, B, C), it is not uncommon for some trusts to own 5, 10, or more such properties. In this case, you use multiple forms. You sequentially number the forms, and re-alphabetize the preprinted vertical columns as D, E, F; G, H, I; J, K, L . . . etc. For each parcel of rental/royalty property, there must be a separate columnar display of income, expenses, and depreciation (or depletion in the case of natural resource property). When each property is fully accounted for, care is required to extend all entries through to ONE total column at the far right. We try to portray this one total column for you in Figure 10.2.

If the trust owns farm property which is being rented or share-cropped, an entirely different form is required. This is **Form 4835: *Farm Rental Income and Expenses*.** Its arrangement is similar to that of Schedule E, Part I. However, it has additional preprinted income and expense lines which are peculiar to farming operations and subsidy payments. A single Form 4835 can accommodate 100 acres of farm rental land . . . or 100,000 acres. The trust can own the land and rent it to other persons or entities in proprietorship, partnership, corporation, or LLC form.

Pooled Investment Activities

Real estate is capital intensive. This generally means that a single trust doesn't have the financial resources to engage in large projects such as apartment buildings, shopping malls, superstores, prestigious hotels, yacht harbors, off-shore mining, and the like. Participation in these projects requires that the trust pool some of its money with that of other investors (of all types).

Pooled investments are more beneficial through pass-through entities such as partnerships, S corporations, other trusts, and real estate mortgage investment conduits (REMICs). While a trustee exercises no direct supervision of these entities, one must always be leery of the marketing hype often associated with pooled-investment projects. Seek only those which are *income* oriented rather than tax shelter oriented.

One of the advantages of pass-through entity investment projects is that, in addition to income distributions, there are also distributions of certain deductions, credits, and capital gains (and losses). These and other pass-through features derive from the fact that partnerships, S corporations, other trusts, and REMICs are not taxable entities. This is unlike investing in large C corporations where, primarily, dividends only are paid.

Distributions from pass-through entities are reported to the IRS — then to you as trustee — on the following official forms (or their substitutes):

Partnership: *Schedule K-1 (1065)* — Partner's Share of Income, Credits, Deductions, etc.

S Corporation: *Schedule K-1 (1120S)* — Shareholder's Share of Income, Credits, Deductions, etc.

Other Trust: *Schedule K-1 (1041)* — Beneficiary's Share of Income, Deductions, Credits, etc.

REMIC: *Schedule Q (1066)* — Notice to Residual Interest Holder of Taxable Income or Net Loss Allocation

All of these information returns are pulled together and entity identified on Schedule E (1040), Parts II, III, and IV. This is the same Schedule E (1040) that you attach to the trust's Form 1041 when directly owning rental and royalty property. The only difference is that the trust's directly owned property is identified in Part I, whereas the indirectly owned property is identified in Parts II, III, and IV. We schematize the reporting arrangement for you in Figure 10.3. Notice the entry in Part V: Net Farm Rentals. The grand total is entered as one figure on page 1 of Form 1041:

Rents, royalties, partnerships, other estates and trusts, etc. Attach Schedule E (Form 1040).

Transactional Gains & Losses

A "transaction" is the sale or exchange of property — trust property in our case. The property may be corporate stock, mutual fund shares, long-term bonds, residential real estate, commercial real estate, farm land, natural resource land, machinery and equipment, collectibles (works of art, coins, guns, stamps, antiques, etc.) . . . and anything else whose unit value varies over time. It is

Sch. E (1040)	SUPPLEMENTAL INCOME AND LOSS		Page 2
Part II	Partnerships & S Corporations		Special Rules
	Description of Entity	INCOME	LOSS
A			
B			
C			
D			
E			
Part III	Estates & Trusts		
A			
B			
Part IV	Real Estate Mortgage Conduits		
A			
B			
Part V	Summary (including Part I)		
Form 4835: Net Farm Rentals			
Transfer: Net from Part I			
	Totals		< >
	NET INCOME OR LOSS ➤		

Fig. 10.3 - Other Forms of Property Holdings on Schedule E (1040), Page 2

because of value variations over time that a transactional event produces gain, no gain/no loss, or loss.

For trust tax accounting, there are two distinct categories of transactional events. The first category is **Schedule D**: *Capital Gains and Losses*; the second category is **Form 4797**: *Ordinary Gains and Losses*. What's the difference?

The difference is that Form 4797 events involve business-use property where *depreciation* or *depletion* has been claimed as a deduction allowance over the years of productive ownership. These allowances apply to rental real estate, natural resource deposits, trucks and tractors, breeder animals, fruit trees and vines, etc.

If, during the year, an item of business property is sold, the procedure is to prepare Form 4797 first, then Schedule D. The reason for this is that with business property there is potential for *recapture gain* (Part III of Form 4797). This is a combination of ordinary gain and capital gain. The capital gain portion transfers to

Schedule D, whereas the ordinary gain portion stays on Form 4797. Furthermore, if business property held more than one year results in a capital loss, it converts to an ordinary loss and stays on Form 4797. The ordinary losses on Form 4797 are not subject to any statutory limitation. The overall result is that Form 4797 is more complicated than Schedule D.

Schedule D, however, has some special rules of its own. Net capital gain (short-term or long-term) can be passed through to the beneficiaries, allocably. Net capital loss (short-term or long-term) remains in the trust where it is carried forward from year to year. Only $3,000 of the net loss can be used in a given year. For these reasons, a specially designed Schedule D (1041) for trusts is used.

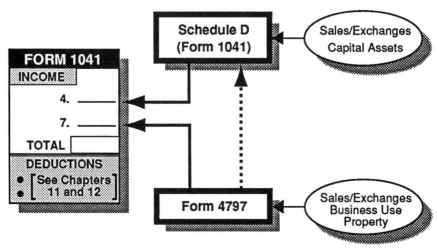

Fig. 10.4 - Attachments to Form 1041 When Making Sales or Exchanges

A schematic representation of the relationship between Schedule D (1041), Form 4797, and Form 1041 is presented in Figure 10.4. As depicted in the figure, when all transactional gain/loss reportings are complete, their totals transfer to the income portion of Form 1041 at the following lines:

4. *Capital gain or <loss>. Attach Schedule D (1041).*
7. *Ordinary gain or <loss>. Attach Form 4797.*

11

COMPREHENDING FORM 1041

As A Producer Of Income, A Trust Must File Annually Form 1041. An Awareness Of This By The Trustor And Near-Mastery Of It By The Trustee Are Indicative Of Prudence And Care. Offsetting Total Income (Before Any Distributions) Are Fiduciary Fees, Legal And Accounting Fees, And Certain Interest And Taxes Paid. If Amounts Are Set Aside Permanently For Charity, An Otherwise Simple Trust Becomes Complex. If So Empowered, The Trustee May Allocate Net Capital Gains (Which Belong To Corpus) To Specific Beneficiaries. When Completed, Form 1041 Must Be Signed By The Trustee: "Under Penalties of Perjury."

In previous chapters, particularly in Chapter 10, we have mentioned Form 1041 and cited its title. But we did not stress its importance nor describe its highlights in any detail. We need to do so now. This is because once the trustors are deceased, each successor trustee is subject to judgment and criticism by family members who are beneficiaries. If the trustee is also a beneficiary, the criticism may turn caustic and accusative. We believe that a properly prepared and timely filed Form 1041 can go a long way towards deflecting any adversarial tendencies that might develop among the beneficiaries.

Even for the simplest and most modest of family trusts, Form 1041 should be prepared by a tax professional. After all, it is an **income tax return**! It is a return that addresses the preservation and distribution of family wealth representing many millions of dollars . . . perhaps up to 100 million or more. With increased wealth in a trust, uninformed beneficiaries often stray from recognizing the basic role of a trust. To reduce the straying, the return preparer can be used as an explainer (to the beneficiaries) of what is required for tax accounting purposes and why it is required.

In this chapter, we do not want to venture too deeply into the "wealth effect" on the complexity of a trust. Instead, we want to focus more down to earth. We want to stress the importance and usefulness of Form 1041, its general format and content, its administrative and distributive deductions, the unusual role of Schedule D (Form 1041) in transactional activities, and "related taxpayer" rules which seek to avoid abuses of the trust by those "clever beneficiaries" and their advisors.

The official instructions to Form 1041 comprise 32 pages . . . or approximately 38,000 words! Obviously, we have to be selective in what we present. Although every trustor should be aware that a Form 1041 has to be prepared after his or her demise, our primary target (in this chapter) is the family member trustee who wants to get a comprehensive "handle" on what Form 1041 is all about.

Head Portion Distinctions

The quickest way for a trustee to gain familiarity with Form 1041 is for us to introduce and discuss its head portion. When we do this, you'll note an immediate difference between Forms 1040 and 1041. The 1041 headmatter is much less self-explanatory than the corresponding head portion of 1040. A glance at Figure 11.1 will tell you why.

The first thing you note in Figure 11.1 is the title: *U.S. Income Tax Return for Estates and Trusts*. This title signifies dual use, which can cause confusion. But, as pointed out previously, two separate returns are involved. An Estate 1041 starts and ends at a different time, and for a different purpose, than does a Trust 1041. Our concern here is the use of Form 1041 strictly for trust return purposes.

Except for the trust name and trustee's block, all other head portion blocks in Figure 11.1 are referenced with a capital letter designation: A through G. Do not confuse these cap-letter

FORM 1041	U.S. INCOME TAX RETURN for ESTATES & TRUSTS	Year

A Type of Entity

☐ Decedent's estate
☐ Simple trust
☐ Complex trust
☐ Grantor trust
☐ Bankruptcy estate
☐ Pooled income fund

Name of Trust:

(If grantor trust, see instructions)

Name of Fiduciary:

Street or P.O. Box Address:

City, State, & ZIP:

C Entity EIN Number

D Date Entity Created

E Nonexempt charitable and split-interest trusts

☐ Sec. 4947 (a)(1)
☐ Not a private foundation
☐ Sec. 4947 (a)(2)

B Number of Schedules K-1 attached ▶

F Check applicable boxes

☐ Initial return
☐ Final return
☐ Amended return

Change in Fiduciary's ▶ ☐ Name ☐ Address

F Pooled mortgage account

☐ Bought
☐ Sold

Date

Fig. 11.1 - The Head Portion of Form 1041 for Family Trusts

designations with similar letters for Schedules A through J associated with the 1041. The headmatter designations are for referencing Specific Instructions that are found in the general instructions to Form 1041. Incidentally, you should make an effort to obtain a copy of the official Form 1041, its schedules (particularly its Schedule K-1), and its 32 pages of instructions.

Although we showed the headmatter blocks in Figure 11.1, we recap them here because of their importance. In alphabetical sequence, the headblocks (as officially titled) are:

A — Type of entity
B — Number of Schedules K-1
C — Employer identification number
D — Date entity created
E — Nonexempt charitable and split-interest trusts
F — Check applicable boxes
G — Pooled mortgage account

We'll skip Block A for the moment, and quickly run through blocks B through G.

Block B is simply a space for entering the number of beneficiaries of the trust. Each must receive separately a Schedule K-1 (to be discussed in Chapter 12). Block C is the Tax ID number that you applied for using Form SS-4 (discussed in Chapter 8). Block D is date that the trust took possession of all trust-assigned property and started earning income. (This was also discussed in Chapter 8.)

Block E, usually, is inapplicable to family trusts. Block E is for those highly funded trusts ($100,000,000 or more), which are partly charitable, partly noncharitable, and partly private foundation types. Special excise taxes apply for political expenditures, excess business holdings, jeopardizing charitable purposes, undistributed income, and other self-dealings under an arrangement for being a charitable remainder entity. These are committee-type entities, the trustees of which are unlikely to be reading this book.

Block F: Initial return ☐ Final return ☐ or Amended return ☐. Check the appropriate box when applicable. Certainly, the first time you file a Trust 1041 return, you must check the "Initial" box.

Block G applies only if the trust bought or sold "certificates of participation" in Federal National Mortgage Association trusts. Such FNMA trusts themselves are tax exempt, but any earnings from your participation in them are not tax exempt.

Type of Entity Checkboxes

Block A in Figure 11.1 lists six separate checkboxes under the item: Type of Entity. With some quick comments, we can eliminate four of the six checkboxes. Elimination derives from the IRS instructions which say—

Check the appropriate box that describes the entity for which you [the fiduciary of the trust] *are filing the return.*

The implication is that you can check only one box for each tax year.

The four checkboxes that are inapplicable here are: Decedent's estate, Grantor trust, Bankruptcy estate, and Pooled income fund.

Eliminating "decedent's estate" reinforces the premise that you cannot have both an Estate 1041 and a Trust 1041 at the same time.

For family trust concerns, a "grantor trust" is inapplicable. In the IRS's words—

*A grantor type trust is a legal trust under applicable state law that is **not recognized** as a separate taxable entity for income tax purposes **because the grantor or other substantial owners have not relinquished complete dominion and control** over the trust.* [Emphasis added.]

The "grantor trust" concept is a generic term that rules out virtually all variants of revocable and reversionary trusts created after March 1, 1986. On this point, the 1041 instructions say—

*Do not report on Form 1041 the income that is taxable to the grantor or another person . . . **who retains a more than 5% interest in any portion** of a trust.*

We discussed the rules on grantor trusts in considerable detail in Chapter 9. Grantor trusts are viewed as having abusive intent. We are simply avoiding grantor trusts altogether.

Two other checkboxes can also be eliminated quickly: Bankruptcy Estate and Pooled Income Fund. Only individuals and corporations can file for bankruptcy: trusts cannot. A trust doesn't go bankrupt; it terminates. A pooled income fund is a charitable remainder trust where the charity itself is the trustee of the trust property. Such trust can accept property from multiple unrelated donors. Professional trustees (working full time) are engaged to administer the "split interests" of the charity and the life estate of each donor. This is not the kind of trust applicable here.

Simple vs. Complex Trusts

The above eliminations leave only two remaining likely checkboxes in Block A of Form 1041. These two are:

☐ Simple trust, OR ☐ Complex trust.

The term "simple" or "complex" as applied to Trust 1041s describes their tax distinctions only. The distinction depends on what the trust instrument directs the trustee to do. Both trust forms are irrevocable; the distinction is how and when the income and corpus are distributed.

On this point, the 1041 instructions say—

A trust may qualify as a simple trust if:

1. The trust instrument requires that all income be distributed currently;

2. The trust instrument does not provide that any amounts are to be paid, permanently set aside, or used for charitable purposes; and

3. The trust does not distribute amounts allocated to the corpus of the trust.

On the subject of complex trusts, the 1041 instructions say—

A complex trust is any trust that does not qualify as a simple trust as explained above.

Thus, a complex trust is simpler in concept than a simple trust. Sounds weird, doesn't it?

The IRS computer knows the difference. Therefore, do not casually check the "complex trust" box out of misunderstanding whether you qualify as a simple trust or not. When in doubt, always check ☐ *Simple trust*. If this turns out to be wrong, you can amend the return later (by so signifying in Block F).

There is one dominant distinguishing feature of a simple trust. It is the requirement that all current income be distributed to designated beneficiaries. The term "current" means at least once annually. The term "all income" does not mean all gross income; it means all *taxable* income. By distributing all taxable income of the trust to the beneficiaries, they pay the tax. The trust nets out with zero taxable income, and therefore zero tax. It is in this sense that the trust is "simple." There are no after-tax accumulations which increase the corpus/capital of the trust.

Trust Administration Deductions

There is a total of seven types of administrative deductions allowed against the total (taxable) income of the trust. The seven are preprinted on page 1 of Form 1041, starting immediately following the line labeled: *Total income.* The deductions are listed in a separate portion of the 1041 bold-designated as: **Deductions.**

As preprinted and listed, the seven deductions are—

1. Interest
2. Taxes
3. Fiduciary fees
4. Charitable deduction
5. Attorney, account, and return preparer fees
6. Other deductions NOT subject to 2% floor
7. Miscellaneous deductions SUBJECT to 2% floor

Of the above deductions, the most frustrating are items 6 and 7. Both make reference to a "2% floor." The 2% floor is one of those gimmicky laws that Congress passed in 1986 at the insistence of the IRS. The objective is to curtail the use of miscellaneous deductions that would otherwise reduce tax revenue to government. The specific law on point is Section 67: *2-Percent Floor on Miscellaneous Itemized Deductions.* Its subsection (a) is the general rule, which reads—

In the case of an individual, the miscellaneous itemized deductions for any taxable year shall be allowed only to the extent that the aggregate of such deductions exceeds 2 percent of adjusted gross income.

Note that this subsection addresses only individuals. Other subsections address other classes of filers. Subsection (e), for example, addresses estates and trusts. The Section 67(e) title is: *Determination of Adjusted Gross Income in Case of Estates and*

Trusts. Trying to interpret this subsection for Form 1041 purposes is much too frustrating. Apply the 2% to the total income, and reduce all incidental, nonspecific expenses by said amount. When dealing with miscellaneous-type trust expenses, it is better to err on the conservative side. This practice cuts down on random suspicions.

One of the simplest deductions to understand is interest paid on trust debt: item 1 above. If it is investment or business-type interest which has not been deducted elsewhere on schedules and attachments to Form 1041, it is a deduction on page 1. This means that the trust has borrowed money to conduct some of its activities. We caution you, though, that too much and too frequent borrowing can jeopardize the perception of you as a prudent trustee.

The deduction for taxes paid (item 2 above) is quite limited. It is limited to—

1. Real estate taxes,
2. State and local income taxes, and
3. The generation-skipping transfer tax imposed on income distributions from the trust.

The most common of these three deductibles is real estate taxes. These are property taxes paid or incurred during the year that are not deductible elsewhere on Form 1041. For example, property taxes paid on bare land, on a qualified residence or on other nonincome-producing realty would be deductible.

Fiduciary Fees

A "fiduciary" is usually the trustee. It may also be some other responsible person assigned by the probate court to administer the trust estate, should the trustee be unable to serve or is under challenge for performance of his duties.

The instructions to Form 1041 put it this way:

A fiduciary is a trustee of a trust . . . or other person in possession of property of a decedent's estate. A fiduciary takes title to property for the purpose of protecting or conserving it for the beneficiaries. The fiduciary (or one of the joint fiduciaries) must file Form 1041 for a domestic trust taxable under Section 641 [Imposition of Tax on Estates and Trusts].

Normally, fiduciaries are paid compensation for their services. Thus, the fiduciary/trustee is entitled to reasonable compensation for performing his trust duties. The amount of compensation authorized should be spelled out in the trust instrument. This authorization is especially important in the case of family trusts where the trustee is not only a family member, but also possibly a beneficiary. The "spelling out" could be along the following lines:

> Each successor trustee shall be entitled to reasonable compensation for services rendered. The amount for "services rendered" shall be based on an hourly rate of $X per hour, unless some other rate is agreed to by a majority of the beneficiaries. For the total hours claimed, the trustee shall keep a timely log on the actual hours devoted to this Trust's activities throughout each taxable year. At any time, a trustee may decline compensation, if he or she chooses.

As per item 3 above, all fiduciary fees are recognized as a deductible administrative expense of the trust. Although deductible by the trust, the amount of compensation itself is **not** tax free to its recipient. It is taxable on a fiduciary's own Form 1040.

As the fiduciary, the trustee must prepare and file Form 1041, with all of its required attachments. In addition, he must also prepare and file **Form 1099-MISC:** *Miscellaneous Income.* This form lists the trust's Tax ID as the payer, and the trustee's name and social security number as the recipient/payee. This "information return" is required whenever the trust pays the fiduciary $600 or more in a given year. The amount paid is entered in the box labeled: *Nonemployee compensation.* The fiduciary is not an employee of the trust. As such, he is not subject to employer withholdings.

However, on the fiduciary's own personal Form 1040, he is subject to income tax **and** self-employment tax on his nonemployee compensation. If the fiduciary is a trustee for several continuous years, he could report his Form 1099-MISC income on Schedule C-EZ: *Net Profit from Business.* On the Schedule C-EZ, he can claim his own expenses up to $2,500 per year. This could include any miscellaneous trust expenses that he did not claim on Form 1041. In effect, the unable-to-claim expenses on Form 1041 may well come out of the compensation paid to the fiduciary.

Charitable Deduction

Ordinarily, a simple trust does not claim a charitable deduction. This is because the trust instrument, either by statement or implication, requires that all or most of the net income generated be distributed to living beneficiaries. In some cases, though, the instrument may provide the trustee with discretionary powers to make certain limited contributions. The limitations are based on some "not to exceed" specified percentage of current income, or on the express desires of one or more beneficiaries (in memory of a deceased beneficiary).

Complex trusts, on the other hand, are required — mandated — to set aside certain amounts of current income (and current corpus) for charitable remainder purposes. The "charitable remainder" is established by actuarial factors of life expectancy of specific beneficiaries. The overall effect is that the designated beneficiary gets an income for life from the trust, part of which is taxable and part of which is nontaxable. The applicable tax rules for accomplishing this are very complicated. Recourse to Section 642(c) and its voluminous regulations is required. This section is titled: *Deduction for Amounts Paid or Permanently Set Aside for a Charitable Purpose*. The amount of deduction by the trust in a given year is unlimited, so long as the total accumulation of prior year set asides computationally meets the actuarial fraction required. Furthermore, the remainder contribution may be made to either a domestic or foreign charity. Recall our discussion in Chapter 6 re charitable remainders.

A synopsis of deduction computations required (exclusive of actuarial factors) is presented in Figure 11.2. Note that the listed line entries are designated as Schedule A (1041). This is a preprinted schedule at the top of page 2 of Form 1041 titled: *Charitable Deduction*. A headnote to this preprinted schedule says—

Do not complete for a simple trust.

Schedule A (1041)	CHARITABLE DEDUCTION

For Amounts Paid or Permanently Set Aside for Charitable Purposes

1. Paid or set aside from gross income _____
2. **Allocable tax-exempt income** < >
3. SUBTRACT line 2 from line 1 _____
4. Capital gains allocated to corpus _____
5. ADD lines 3 and 4 _____
6. Sec. 1202 capital gain exclusion < >
7. SUBTRACT line 6 from line 5 ⟶ [   ]

ENTER HERE AND ON PAGE 1 OF FORM 1041

Fig. 11.2 - Entries Required for Computing Charitable Deduction

In addition, the official instructions say—

Certain trusts may claim a deduction from gross income for amounts permanently set aside for a charitable purpose . . . [providing] *the set aside amounts* [are] *required by the terms of the trust instrument. . . . Further, the trust instrument must provide for an irrevocable remainder interest to be transferred to or for the use of* [one or more] *specific charitable organizations described in Section 170(c)* [Charitable Contribution Defined]. *. . . Trusts that claim a charitable deduction* [under Section 642(c)] *must also file Form 1041-A* [U.S. Information Return; Trust Accumulation of Charitable Amounts].

The one item that we want to call to your attention in Figure 11.2 is line 2. It is labeled: *Tax-exempt income allocable to charitable contributions.* Because the beneficiaries who share in the charitable remainder interests get a tax benefit, the trust deduction has to be reduced allocably. For determining the amount of this reduction, the instructions at line 2 say—

Multiply line 1 by a fraction, the numerator of which is the total tax-exempt income of the trust, and the denominator of which is the [combined taxable and tax-exempt] *gross income of the*

trust. Do not include in the denominator any losses allocated to corpus.

Another item for attention in Figure 11.2 is line 6. It is officially labeled: *Section 1202 exclusion allocable to capital gains paid or permanently set aside for charitable purposes.* The "Section 1202" is a 50% exclusion of capital gain from the sale of certain small business stock. When applicable, said amount is already a deduction. Consequently, it has to be "backed out" from its capital gain portion included in line 4. Otherwise, there would be a double deduction effect on the charitable deduction computation.

Legal & Accounting Fees

Unless the trustee asserts firm control over his/her family trust affairs, legal, accounting, and return preparer fees can get out of hand. This is because professionals tend to take advantage of trusts. Philosophically, trust property is viewed by professionals as "dead persons' money." This view eases any conscience guilt and can lead to fee milking by aggressive professionals. If a trust has $10,000,000 in assets, for example, a $10,000 fee (which is 1/10th of 1%) would not seem exorbitant. But, based on the amount of time a professional actually spent on the task — say, several or so hours — the fee would indeed be exorbitant. Rarely will such persons discuss their fee openly and candidly. Just be aware of this fact. Those fees which are ordinary and necessary for bona fide trust administration purposes are deductible in full.

Deductible legal fees are those which apply to the trust administration process overall. This usually involves dispute letters, contract interpretation, and probate-type court proceedings. Some creditor or injured party may have a claim against the trust. The titling and ownership of trust property may be unclear. There may be a conflict of interest between two or more beneficiaries. Or, the trustee may be under attack for some perceived malfeasance of duty. Where legal fees related to specific property holdings, such as rental real estate involving the eviction of tenants and processing of insurance claims, those fees attach directly to the income and expense accounting of the property itself.

Bookkeeping and accounting fees that relate to specific business activities are part of the expenses attributable to those activities. Example are the preparation of income and expense spreadsheets (weekly, monthly, quarterly) for Schedules C (proprietorships), E-I (real estate rentals), E-II (partnerships and S corporations), and F (farm income or loss). These fees are deductible directly on said schedules rather than on Form 1041. However, if some "certified" accounting of the overall receipts and disbursements of the trust is required, the fees paid would be a 1041 item. Except for unusual circumstances, most trustees themselves do the banking, investing, checkwriting, and other general accounting chores.

Probably the most straightforward 1041 fee deductions are payments to tax return preparers. Form 1041 and all of its required attachments are prepared once a year. The effort includes all corresponding forms and schedules for instate and outstate filings. Said fees also include the preparation of information returns (W-2s, 1099s, K-1s, etc.); the preparation for and representation at IRS audits and appeals; and as a witness in Tax Court proceedings.

Investment advisory fees, property appraisal fees, financial counseling fees, and business consultation fees, are deductible elsewhere. They are *not* deductible as attorney, accountant, and return preparer fees. Property appraisals add to the cost basis of the property appraised. Business consulting fees are deductible on Schedules C, E, or F. Investment advisory and financial counseling fees are deductible as miscellaneous expenses under the 2% floor.

The "where" of professional fee deductions can be perplexing. Particularly so, if the trustee is overly dependent on professionals and allows them to run the affairs. Nevertheless, Figure 11.3 is intended as a helpful guideline when the fees become unduly pervasive.

Other Items of Note

In addition to what has been discussed, Form 1041 consists of the following schedules:

Schedule B — *Income Distribution Deduction*
— we'll discuss this in Chapter 12

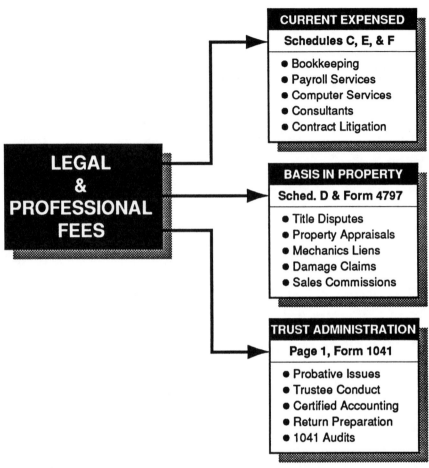

Fig. 11.3 - Caution When Assigning Professional Fees as Trust Expenses

Schedule G — *Tax Computation*
— more or less self-explanatory, but not as important for simple trusts as it is for complex trusts

Schedule I — *Alternative Minimum Tax*
— a further attempt to discourage the use of trusts as private tax shelters, and to discourage the trust from engaging aggressively in commercial tax shelters

Schedule J — *Accumulated Distribution for Certain Complex Trusts*

— required only for trusts created before March 1, 1984 or where a trust has been previously treated as a foreign trust

On page 2 of Form 1041, lower portion, there is a batch of nine checkbox questions captioned as: *Other Information.* six of the nine questions are to be answered either "Yes" ☐ or "No" ☐. If "Yes," explanatory details are required. In abbreviated form, the six questions relate to—

1. Tax-exempt income (discussed in Chapter 10).
2. Assignment to the trust of any personal service income (possible indicator of abusive trust activities; trust may be invalidated).
3. Signature authority over foreign financial accounts (if over $10,000 special information reporting required).
4. Transfers of trust property to a foreign trust (if so, additional reporting forms required).
5. Mortgage interest income from trust-financed residence sales or loans (requires name and SSN of each payee; if family member, explain).
6. Present or future trust beneficiaries who are "skip persons" (discussed in Chapter 9).

There are three non-Yes/No questions which read:

7. *If this is a complex trust making the section 663(b) election, check here* ▶ ☐. This is an election to treat any amount paid or credited to a beneficiary within 65 days following the close of the tax year as being paid or credited on the last day of that tax year.

8. *To make a section 643(e)(3) election, attach Schedule D (Form 1041), and check here* ▶ ☐. This election pertains to the distribution of "property in kind" from the trust to a beneficiary, whereby the trust recognizes gain as if the property were sold to the beneficiary at its fair market value.

9. *If the decedent's estate has been open for more than 2 years, attach an explanation for the delay in closing the estate, and check here* ▶ ☐. This is further recognition of the fact that a trustor's estate after the trustor's death is a separate entity apart from the family trust.

Capital Gains & Losses

The real test of one's comprehension of Form 1041 is knowing how to treat capital gains and losses in trust affairs. Much of the property in a significant family trust consists of capital assets. The principal examples are corporate stock, real estate, natural resources (timber, mines, wells) and collectibles (coins, stamps, antiques, paintings). Other capital assets include partnership interests, business goodwill, technology patents, vehicles, and equipment. Capital assets plus noncapital assets (interest-bearing accounts, inventory for sale to customers, copyrights, accounts receivable) constitute the corpus property of a trust.

When a capital asset of a trust is sold at a gain, the capital gain therewith is part of the corpus property. And, so too, is capital loss therewith. For example, suppose the trust held 3,560 shares of XYZ mutual fund of corporate stock. When transferred to the trust irrevocably, the shares were valued at $100,000. The $100,000 is trust corpus (also called: "trust principal"). If the shares were sold for $165,000, the $65,000 gain would also be trust corpus or principal. If the shares were sold for $75,000, the $25,000 loss would also be trust corpus or principal. What does the tax law say about the treatment of capital gains and losses in trust property transactions?

Answer: IRC Section 643(a)(3): *Distributable Net Income; Capital Gains and losses.* This section reads—

*Gains from the sale or exchange of capital assets **shall be excluded to the extent that** such gains are allocated to corpus and are not (A) paid, credited, or required to be distributed to any beneficiary during the taxable year, or (B) paid, permanently set aside, or to be used for* [charitable] *purposes.*

*Losses from the sale or exchange of capital assets **shall be excluded, except to the extent** such losses are taken into account in determining the amount of gains from the sale or exchange of capital assets which are paid, credited, or required to be distributed to any beneficiary during the taxable year.* [Emphasis added.]

The essence of Section 643(a)(3) is that, unless the trust instrument specifically requires that net capital gains if any, be distributed to one or more beneficiaries (or to charity), or allows the trustee reasonable distributive discretion therewith, said gains shall be retained in the trust. In no event, shall net capital losses be distributed to beneficiaries (or to charity).

Section 643(a)(3) puts the burden squarely on the trustor to establish his corpus distributive intent clearly in his trust instrument. His alternatives in this regard might be:

One — Prohibit the distribution of any capital gains except in cases of dire financial need by one or more beneficiaries.

Two — Limit the distribution of capital gain and corpus property to some fixed percentage amount per year (5%, 10%, or whatever).

Three — Empower the trustee with reasonable discretion to allocate all capital gains as he/she best sees fit, such that the trust will continue in operation for a set minimum number of years (10, 20, or whatever).

Obviously, when distributing capital gains and/or other corpus property, the ability of the trust to generate income diminishes correspondingly. Much depends on the distributive and terminative intent of the crating trustors.

Schedule D (1041) Allocations

Let us assume that a trustee has reasonable discretion in the allocation of net capital gains. How would he/she go about making the allocation?

FAMILY TRUSTS & TRUSTORS

This is where Schedule D (Form **1041**) comes in. You already know that there is a Schedule D (Form 1040). Parts I (short-term) and II (long-term) of Schedules D 1040 and 1041 are nearly identical. These parts involve the netting of gains and losses short-term, and the netting of gains and losses long-term. The Part III of the Schedules D differ significantly.

It is Part III of Schedule D (1041) where allocations between beneficiaries and the trust take place. The caption here is: *Summary of Parts I and II*. Part III is arranged in three columns as shown in Figure 11.4. As can be noted in said figure, column (1) is the allocation to *Beneficiaries*; column (2) is the allocation to the *Trust*; and column (3) is the *Total* of both columns.

Schedule D (1041)	CAPITAL GAINS & LOSSES		Part III
ALLOCATION OF PARTS I & II	(1) Beneficiaries	(2) The Trust	(3) Total
1 Net short-term gain <loss>			
2 28% rate gain <loss>			
3 Unrecaptured Sec. 1250 gain			
4 Net long-term gain <loss>			
5 Total net gain or <loss>	(A)	(B)	
(A) may be gain only. (B) may be gain or loss; loss limited to $3,000.			

Fig. 11.4 - The Allocation of Capital Gains or Losses by a Trust

Also note in Figure 11.4 that there are five horizontal entry lines. The fifth such line is: *Total net gain or <loss>*. Below this total line (on the official Schedule D) there are some preprinted instructions on what to do.

If the total line of column (1) is net capital gain, that amount passes through proportionately to designated beneficiaries. Except for the termination year of the trust, no capital losses pass through to the beneficiaries. Therefore, the Total line of column (1) cannot be a loss . . . ordinarily. All capital losses are borne by the trust.

If the Total line of column (2) is a net capital gain, the trust pays tax on such gain. If this column is a net capital loss, the trust allowable current year loss is limited to $3,000. Any capital loss in excess of $3,000 is carried forward to subsequent years of the trust.

Suspect Transactions

A family trust with 5 million, 50 million, or more millions of dollars in assets is a tempting target for professionals, beneficiaries, distant relatives, and nonfamily associates of the trustee. The temptation is to perceive the trust property and capital as a close private financial institution. Such a perception leads to wheeling and dealing in questionable transactions which regulated commercial institutions would not likely consider. Hence, there are certain restrictions on transactions between related taxpayers. The tax law on point is Section 267: *Losses, Expenses, and Interest with Respect to Transactions Between Related Taxpayers.*

In essence, Section 267 limits the tax recognition of certain gains and losses between a trust and its related persons. The instructions to Schedule D (1041) state that—

*A trust cannot deduct a loss from the sale or exchange of property **directly or indirectly** between any of the following:*

- *A grantor [trustor] and a fiduciary [trustee] of a trust;*
- *A fiduciary and a fiduciary or beneficiary of another trust created by the same grantor;*
- *A fiduciary and a beneficiary of the same trust; or*
- *A trust fiduciary and a corporation of which more than 50% in value of the outstanding stock is owned directly or indirectly by or for the trust or by or for the grantor of the trust.*

As an illustration of the prohibitions above, the case of *B.S. Meek*, CA-9, 98-1 USTC ¶ 50,179 is instructive. The Meeks created a trust for the exclusive benefit of their grandchildren. They designated two unrelated persons (McCormick and Furman), who were unrelated to the Meeks, to be trustees of the trust. The Meeks "sold" to the trust a limited partnership interest at a substantial capital loss. The trustees, from their own funds, paid a nominal amount for the virtually worthless partnership interest. Why two strangers would do this for someone else's grandchildren certainly raises suspicions of its own. The intent, of course, was to create the illusion of an independent trust.

The Meeks claimed a large capital loss on their 1991 tax return. Being well in excess of $3,000, they had a large capital loss carryover to 1992. In 1992, they sold other property (outside of the trust) for a substantial capital gain. The capital loss carryover and the 1992 capital gain essentially nullified each other. This nullity meant that there was no income tax consequence to the Meeks. The Meeks then transferred the capital gains proceeds to the trust, but, as grantors, paid no transfer tax thereon.

Under the provisions of subsections 267(a)(1): *Deduction for losses disallowed* and 267(d)(4): *Relationship between grantor and fiduciary of a trust*, the IRS disallowed the entire Meek cycle of transactions. The 9th Circuit Court of Appeals upheld the IRS's position. The Court's holding confirms the point that a family trust is NOT a device for engaging in tax subterfuge.

In most respects, therefore, all property transactions between a family trust and its related persons are suspect. Not only are such transactions tax suspect, they are suspect by those beneficiaries who do not participate in the transactions. The suspect rules reinforce the primary purpose of every family trust. That purpose, in its purest form, is to distribute income and corpus. Until all proper distributions are made, the trust property must be preserved and maintained . . . diligently and prudently.

Always keep in mind that a fiduciary/trustee must sign and date Form 1041. Said signature appears directly under the preprinted jurat clause:

Under penalties of perjury, I declare that I have examined this return, including accompanying schedules and statements, and to the best of my knowledge and belief, it is true, correct, and complete.

12

HOW DISTRIBUTIONS MADE

Most Family Trusts Seek To Distribute INCOME Annually And CORPUS Occasionally Over Extended Periods Of Time. Simple Trusts Must Distribute Income Currently Whereas Complex Trusts May Accumulate Income For Specific Purposes. The Total Distributable Income Is Computed On Schedule B (1041), After Which It Is Shared Among All Beneficiaries On Schedules K-1 (1041). That Income Which Is Deducted By The Trust On Its Form 1041 IS INCLUDED ALLOCABLY On Each Beneficiary's Own Form 1040. There Are 6 Blank Lines On A K-1 For Noting Distributions Of Exempt Income And Distributions Of Corpus Cash.

The purpose of a genuine family trust, as we've said so many times earlier, is to distribute *income* to the beneficiaries and, ultimately, to distribute all *corpus* (property or principal) to them. A family trust is neither a tax shelter nor a wealth preserver forever. Ordinarily, the income is distributed annually, whereas corpus is distributed whenever the need arises or as directed by the trust instrument. The manner of making these distributions is determined by the following "activity modes"—

[1] Scrutinizing the trust instrument for mandatory and discretionary intent of the trustor(s).
[2] Distinguishing the trust as "simple" or "complex" for each distributable year.
[3] Determining the distributable net income of the trust.

[4] Using Schedule K-1 (1041) for making — and recording — the distributions to each beneficiary.
[5] Identifying "skip persons" in a GST (generation-skipping trust) when portions of taxable corpus are distributed.

We are taking the position in this chapter of addressing only "how" the distributions are made. The taxation details of the trust and the taxation details of each recipient beneficiary are not addressed. If the trustor and trustee each knows what needs to be done distributionwise, professional tax preparers can — and probably should — be sought.

Accordingly, in this our final chapter, we want to address the activity modes listed above, and show how they fit into the scheme of things. After all, distributing income and corpus from a family trust is an ongoing affair for many years. In this regard, the "how" is more important to a trustor than the day-to-day operations of the trust. Knowing the how before a trustor dies can make for better trust enjoyment by all those family members who follow.

Candidate Distribution Sources

Strictly for overview purposes, let us make an assumption. The trustor has empowered the trustee with "sole and exclusive discretion" over the arrangement, management, and distribution of all trust income and corpus. We do not recommend such unlimited power: it's too easy to abuse. Still, our assumption is that the trustee is in a position to distribute to the beneficiaries as much as he can, prudently and meaningfully. As such, what would be his range of distribution sources?

We can see five different classes of distribution sources. As depicted in Figure 12.1, the five sources are: (1) exempt income, (2) ordinary income, (3) capital gains, (4) corpus cash (money), and (5) corpus property (other than cash). The term "corpus cash" is after-tax money retained by the trust. The term "property other than cash" is property in kind held by the trust without its being sold or exchanged.

Looking at Figure 12.1, we want to highlight two features there. One feature is that if any income is retained by the trust, it is taxed to

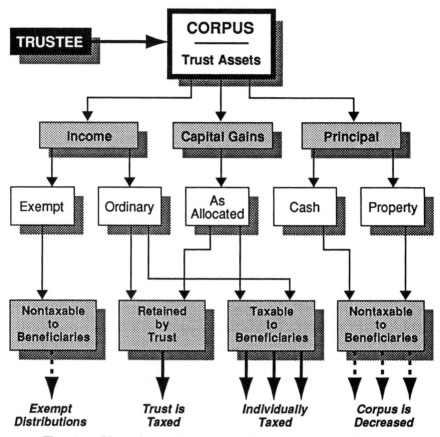

Fig. 12.1 - Discretionary Aspects in Management of Trust Assets

the trust. The trustee may want to retain some of the current year's income for any number of valid reasons. Such reasons might include a cash reserve for guaranteed payments to certain beneficiaries, emergency payments to special needs beneficiaries, major business and property improvements, and new investment opportunities. All after-tax cash retentions revert to the corpus (principal) of the trust.

The second feature in Figure 12.1 to which we call your attention is the distinction between corpus cash and corpus property. The cash portion of corpus consists of—

1. Retained income (for reasons above).

2. Capital gains and losses (where gains are not distributed to beneficiaries.
3. Deductible allowances such as depreciation, depletion, and amortization (which reduce the tax accounting income).
4. Rebates, credits, and refunds of any kind after the close of the taxable year.

When corpus property is distributed, it is usually in the form of stock shares, installment notes, parcels of realty, collectible items, inventory for sale to customers, vehicles and equipment (used in business), and other items which are partitionable for distribution to one beneficiary at a time. When corpus property is distributed, it is treated as the sale or exchange of said property to each recipient beneficiary.

When corpus cash or property is distributed, it reduces the value of the remaining corpus. This places a burden on the trustee to establish a separate set of records for tracking the growth and diminishment of the corpus principal. The trustor and beneficiaries have to rely on the integrity of the trustee to keep such a record. There is no annual tax form, as in the case of trust income, for doing so. (Recall Chapters 10 and 11.) Hence, the most vulnerable area of trust abuse is the partitioning and distribution of corpus assets.

Scrutinizing the Contract

Now that you know what a trustee can do with unlimited power, the real issue is: What are the distribution instructions designated in the trust instrument (the contract)? And, what degree of discretion does the trustee have with regard to each individual beneficiary?

To address these concerns, the trustee must carefully read the contract and try to interpret what it actually means. We are not comfortable with the prospect that the clarity he needs will be there. This is because the trust instrument, if created by husband and wife as trustors, will be front loaded with contingencies and directives on what happens when the first of the trustors dies. The successor trustee wants to look past the first trustor items and focus on those paragraphs which follow the section: *When the Surviving Trustor Dies*. This is the point in time when both trustors are deceased. The time difference may be 5, 10, or 15 years after the trust instrument was first drawn up. Our guess is that the successor beneficiaries and their distributive rights will not be well thought through. Therefore, the trustee has to scrutinize the trust document and set forth his own priorities of what he needs to know and what he needs to do . . . and when he needs to do them.

The first priority is to identify all persons who are expressly named as beneficiaries, those persons unnamed but who are readily identifiable in relation to the named persons (e.g., spouses of the trustor's children, siblings of the trustors), and those now born but who were unborn at the time the trust was prepared. The trustee should write down all names, ages, addresses, phone numbers, and social security numbers. Also, he should ascertain as appropriate from each beneficiary his/her employment status, financial status, educational status, and medical status. This is the kind of background information needed when making decisions on the amount and timing of distributions of income and corpus.

The next priority is to classify all beneficiaries in some orderly and well defined manner. The wording in the contract may be helpful. The classification could be as follows:

A. Those having life interests, in the form of guaranteed income and support.
B. Adult beneficiaries having nonlife interests, due to financial status and occupational levels.
C. Minor children, with or without special needs, and their respective educational goals.
D. Generation-skipping persons and charitable remainders, if any. GST persons and charities require particular tax care.

Once the names and classes of beneficiaries have been sorted from the trust contract, extraction from the contractual language has to be made of the distinction, if any, between mandatory and discretionary distributions of income and corpus. The general tax rule is that within a given class of beneficiaries, all must be treated the same. This generality can be overriden for good cause. Otherwise, discretionary power is usually limited to between classes rather than within a class.

Seek Legal Opinions Early

When dealing with trust assets in excess of 3, 5, 10, 50, or 100 million dollars, the possibility of adversarial litigation is just a hair's-breadth away. At some point, a beneficiary may claim some wrongdoing on the part of the trustee. In many cases, the alleged wrongdoing may originate from a nonbeneficiary relative who has been urged on by a covetous attorney or a critical professional seething at the loss of lucrative fee milking that a wealthy estate attracts. On this possibility, we urge that the trustee prepare to some extent for the "likely inevitable."

Preferably before the first taxable year of the trust, legal opinion should be sought on the extent of the trustee's discretionary powers with respect to each identifiable beneficiary. Opinion(s) should be obtained from an experienced attorney **who did not participate** in the preparation of the trust instrument. It is important to have an independent reading by an attorney in the state and county which has original jurisdiction over the trust contract and its assets.

Perhaps one or more paragraphs from the trust instrument will be truly puzzling to the trustee. He should present the attorney with the specific names of the beneficiaries he is concerned about, then request that his opinion be cited in writing. Of course, such is just one attorney's opinion. But at least it shows a responsible effort to do things right.

Here's a true example of what we mean. The following language is extracted from a family trust which was written 18 years before the surviving trustor died. It reads in selected part—

> Following the Surviving Trustor's death, the Trustee shall distribute such portions of the undistributed income and principal of the Trust, up to the whole thereof, to one or more of the group consisting of the issue of the Trustors, and spouses and surviving spouses of the issue of the Trustors, . . . and the issue of the children of the Trustors, . . . and on such terms and conditions, either outright or in trust, as the Surviving Trustor may appoint in the last unrevoked written and dated instrument amending this Agreement, other than a will.

Surely, you see what we mean. How would you interpret the above? Does the term: "up to the whole thereof" imply any discretionary power with respect to the children of the trustors, the spouses of the children of the trustors, and the issue (born and unborn) of the issue of the children of the trustors? Similarly for the term: "either outright on in trust."

We think a better administrative job can be done after getting at least one legal opinion on the above. Seeking more than two such opinions is not advised. Nevertheless, any fees paid for such opinion(s) are legitimate administrative expenses of the trust, deductible in full against its total income.

The Role of Schedule B (1041)

In order to distribute income from a family trust, there is a particular schedule incorporated directly in Form 1041: *U.S. Income Tax Return for . . . Trusts*. Said schedule appears on page 2 of Form 1041. Its title is: **Schedule B:** *Income Distribution Deduction* (IDD). This title alone implies — or should imply — that whatever income amount is distributed to the beneficiaries is deductible by the trust. Such indeed is the case.

It is a statutory requirement [IRC Sections 652 and 662] that whatever distributable taxable income is deducted by the trust must be included in the taxable income of the beneficiaries. We portray this deduction-inclusion concept for you in Figure 12.2. As you should surmise from this figure, the more income that can be passed through to beneficiaries, the less tax the trust will pay on any retained income. For a given amount of taxable income, the trust tax is about twice that of an individual's tax. For example, if $10,000 of taxable income were retained by the trust, its tax would be $3,000. If the $10,000 were passed through to a married beneficiary, the tax would be $1,500. Consequently, the trustee's goal is to minimize the trust tax as much as possible.

Before shifting any of the trust income to the beneficiaries, Schedule B (1041) must be completed. To do so, requires entries on up to 15 official steps. The final step thereon is that which can be computationally distributed. Some of the steps are self-explanatory and others are not. Those which are not self-explanatory focus on complex trusts, the treatment of capital gains, and the set-asides for charity. This suggests that we revisit the characteristics of simple and complex trusts that we discussed in Chapter 11.

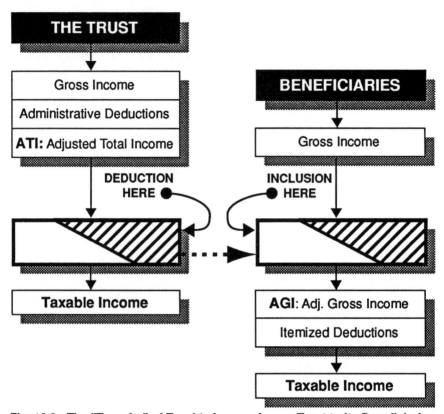

Fig. 12.2 - The "Transfer" of Taxable Income from a Trust to its Beneficiaries

Simple vs. Complex Revisited

Section 651 of the Internal Revenue Code addresses the definitional aspects of simple trusts. This section is officially titled: *Deduction for Trusts Distributing Current Income Only*. Note that the term "simple trust" does not appear in this title. This is because the focus stress is on "distributing current income only."

More directly, Regulation § 1.651(a)-1: *Simple trusts*, describes such trusts as those whose "governing instrument" provides that—

(1) all of its income be distributed currently;
(2) no charitable contribution be made; and
(3) no distributions from corpus be made.

Regulation § 1.651(a)-1(b) goes on to say—

*A trust may be a simple trust for one year and a complex trust for another year. . . .Under Section 651 a trust qualifies as a simple trust in a taxable year in which it is **required** to distribute all of its income currently . . . **whether or not** the distributions of current income are in fact made.* [Emphasis added.]

What income is *required* to be distributed currently?

The answer depends on the terms of the trust instrument and the applicable local law. There is a fair amount of latitude. For example, Regulation § 1.651(a)-2 points out that—

*If the trust instrument provides that the trustee in determining the distributable income shall first **retain a reserve** for depreciation or otherwise make due allowance for keeping the trust corpus intact by retaining a reasonable amount of current income for that purpose, the retention of current income for that purpose **will not disqualify** the trust from being a "simple" trust. . . . It is immaterial, for purposes of determining whether all the income is required to be distributed currently, that the amount of income allocated to a particular beneficiary is not specified in the instrument.* [Emphasis added.]

We think there is wiggle room here to distribute excess corpus cash without jeopardizing the simple trust rules. We'll show how this can be done when we discuss Schedule K-1 (1041) later below. We interpret "no distributions from corpus" to be *property in kind* distributions rather than ordinary cash. Special rules apply when property in kind is distributed from corpus [Sec. 653(e)].

The treatment of complex trusts is addressed in Section 661: *Deduction for Trusts Accumulating Income or Distributing Corpus.* Its subsection (a) reads in significant part—

In any taxable year there shall be allowed as a deduction in computing taxable income of a trust (other than a [simple] trust), the sum of—

(1)   any amount of income . . . required to be distributed currently (including any amount required to be distributed which may be paid out of income or corpus . . .); and

*(2)   any other amount properly paid or credited or required to be distributed for such taxable year; **but** such deduction shall not exceed the distributable net income of the trust.*

From the above citation, you can sense immediately that a complex trust can do far more things than a simple trust. For this greater latitude, though, the clause "shall not exceed" implies greater computational complexity. Indeed it does. When we get to the 15-step computation sequence for the amount of deduction allowed, you'll see what we mean.

In the meantime, we present in Figure 12.3 a bird's eye view of the distributive differences between a simple trust and a complex trust. A point to keep in mind is that a complex trust can always do what a simple trust can do . . . but **not** vice versa. However, for specific events, a simple trust can self-convert to a complex trust for a particular year, then revert back to a simple trust thereafter.

Limitation on Deduction

Section 651 (simple trusts) and Section 661 (complex trusts) both have a limitation imposed on the amount of distribution to beneficiaries that can be deducted from the taxable income of the trust. This is the consequence of the *matching principle* between the deductible income of the trust and the includible income of the beneficiaries. What the trust deducts, the beneficiaries must include. Recall Figure 12.2.

The deduction limitation [Section 651(b)] for simple trusts is more self-explanatory. It reads in full as—

*If the amount of income required to be distributed currently exceeds the distributable net income of the trust for the taxable year, the deduction **shall be limited** to the amount of the **distributable net income**. For this purpose, the **computation** of the distributable income **shall not include items of income*** *which are not included in the gross income of the trust and the deductions allocable thereto.* [Emphasis added.]

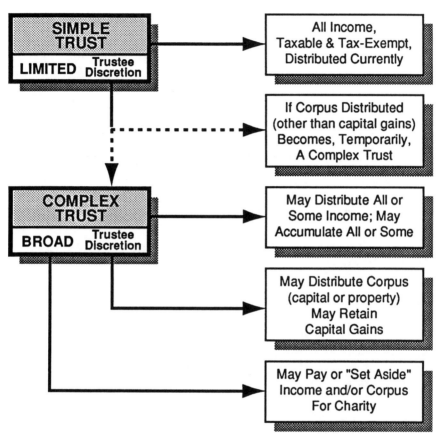

Fig. 12.3 - Comparative Features of "Simple" Trust vs. "Complex" Trust

This citation tells us three things. One: the limitation amount is based on *Distributable Net Income:* DNI. Two: there is a computational process that must be pursued to establish the DNI. The computational process gives priority to those accounting matters required for complex trusts. And, three: the computation excludes sources of income (such as tax-exempt interest and allowances for depreciation and depletion) and deductions which are reflected in adjusted total income of the trust (such as charitable contributions, attorney fees, etc.).

For complex trusts, the DNI limitation above applies. In addition, Section 661(b): *Character of Amounts Distributed*, reads—

> *The amount* [of deduction] *. . . shall be treated as consisting of the same proportion of each class of items entering into the computation of distributable income . . . as the total of each class bears to the total distributable income of the trust, in the absence of the allocation of different classes of income under the specific terms of the governing instrument.*

In complex trusts, the DNI computation involves adjustments for charitable contributions, deductions allocable to tax-exempt interest, capital gains, capital losses, prior income accumulations, allocations to corpus, and special set asides for life beneficiaries, minors, and GST "skip persons."

For a clearer definition of DNI, Regulation §1.643(a)-0 is helpful. It states that—

> *The term "distributable net income" has no application except in the taxation of trusts and their beneficiaries. It limits the deductions allowable to trusts for amounts paid, credited, or required to be distributed to beneficiaries and is used to determine how much of an amount paid, credited, or required to be distributed to a beneficiary will be includible in his gross income It is also used to determine the character of distributions to the beneficiaries.*

The Computational Sequence

The DNI is that which is available for distribution to all beneficiaries, collectively. It is computed on Schedule B (1041): *Income Distribution Deduction*, previously mentioned. We present an abridgment of Schedule B in Figure 12.4. Note that a total of 15 steps is involved.

Steps 1 and 2 represent what we class as the "ordinary income" aspects of trust activities. In contrast, Steps 3 through 6 represent the "capital transactions" of the trust. Capital transactions involve the sale, exchange, or other transformation of corpus assets. Every capital transaction results in either a capital gain, return of capital, or capital loss. Ordinarily, capital transaction results are *excluded* from the concept of DNI. As such, they remain in the trust and are not distributed unless the trust instrument or local law requires their distribution.

Sched. B	INCOME DISTRIBUTION DEDUCTION	Form 1041
1	Adjusted total income (from page 1)	
2	Adjusted tax-exempt interest	
3	Total net gain from Sch. D (1041)	
4	Adjusted charitable deduction from Sch. A (1041)	
5	Capital gains set aside for charity	
6	If capital gain on page 1, enter as negative	
7	**DNI** Combine steps 1 through 6 • If zero or less, enter -0- ▶	
8	Accounting income as per contract	
9	Income required distributed currently	
10	Other amounts paid, credited, or required	
11	Total distributions. Add steps 9 and 10	
12	Tax-exempt income included in step 11	
13	SUBTRACT step 12 from step 11	
14	SUBTRACT step 2 from step 7	
15	**DNI** INCOME DISTRIBUTION DEDUCTION Enter here the SMALLER OF step 13 or step 14 on page 1.	

Fig. 12.4 - Abbreviated Version of Schedule B, Form 1041

Regulation § 1.643(a)-3: *Capital gains and losses,* makes the exclusion-inclusion point clear. Its subregulation (a) reads—

[G]*ains from the sale or exchange of capital assets are* ***ordinarily excluded*** *from distributable net income and are ordinarily not considered as paid, credited, or required to be distributed to any beneficiary* ***unless they are***:

*(1) Allocated to income under the terms of the governing instrument or local law by the fiduciary on its books or **by notice** to the beneficiary.*

*(2) Allocated to corpus and **actually distributed** to beneficiaries during the taxable year, or*

*(3) **Utilized (pursuant** to the terms of the governing instrument or the **practice followed by the fiduciary**) in determining the amount which is distributed or required to be distributed.* [Emphasis added.]

If capital gains are paid, set aside, or used for charitable purposes, said gains must be included in the DNI computation. Otherwise, if capital gains are distributed to noncharitable beneficiaries, they are passed through to them **independent** of any ordinary income. This was the message we were trying to get across in the latter part of Chapter 11, particularly in Figure 11.4.

Steps 8 through 15 in Figure 12.4 seek to establish what portion of the DNI (step 7) is taxable to the beneficiaries. These steps do so by "backing out" any tax-exempt income. Step 8 refers to: *accounting income.* This is whatever the trust instrument says it is. It includes all forms of income for which the trustee has to make an accounting to the beneficiaries, whether distributed, distributable, or not. Step 10: ***Other amounts paid, credited, or required to be distributed***, include—

annuities [guaranteed payments] *to the extent not paid out of income, discretionary distributions of corpus* [cash], *and distributions of property in kind.*

Step 15 is bold captioned: *Income Distribution Deduction* (IDD). This is identical with the caption on Schedule B (1041) itself. An associated instruction reads—

The income distribution deduction determines the amount of income that will be taxed to the beneficiaries.

There you have it! Whatever evolves as the bottom line on Schedule B becomes an allowable distribution deduction against the taxable income of the trust. The exact same amount is mandatorily included in the gross income of the beneficiaries. Where there is more than one beneficiary, the IDD is allocated to each beneficiary in proportion to his or her distributive share of the trust income.

The Beneficiary K-1s

All trust income and corpus (property or principal) must eventually be distributed to the beneficiaries. The distribution is done incrementally, year after year. How is this done? Answer: This is where **Schedule K-1** (Form 1041) comes in.

Schedule K-1 is officially titled: ***Beneficiary's Share of Income, Deductions, Credits, etc.*** Note that this title is singular possessive: Beneficiary's. This implies that there is one Schedule K-1 for each separate beneficiary of a trust. Such, indeed, is the case. A headnote instruction on the K-1 says—

Complete a separate Schedule K-1 for each beneficiary.

When each K-1 is completed, it is known as an "information" return. It is not a tax return, per se. A trustee has no duty to prepare the tax returns of the beneficiaries. But, he does have a duty to furnish *tax information* to each beneficiary, AND to the IRS. The number of K-1s issued is reported in the headportion of Form 1041. Each beneficiary uses the K-1 information to prepare his or her own tax return. The IRS uses the information to computer-match what has been furnished with that which each beneficiary self-reports.

The K-1 has a left-hand side and a right-hand side, each accommodating 38 separate line entries. The left-hand side displays—

Beneficiary's identifying number ▶ _____
Beneficiary's name, address, and ZIP code
Col. (a) *Allocable share item*

Correspondingly, the right-hand side displays—

Trust's identifying number ▶ _____
Fiduciary's name, address, and ZIP code
Col. (b) *Amount*; Col. (c) *Where to enter on Form 1040*

The last six lines of the 38 are blank for nontaxable write-ins: tax-exempt interest, corpus distributions of cash, property distributions in kind, and other items of note which are not income.

Strictly for overview purposes, we present in Figure 12.5 an abbreviated version of Schedule K-1 (Form 1041). It is "abbreviated" only to give you an idea of what a K-1 is all about. You would glean a better appreciation with an official K-1 and its instructions. The instructions permit *substitute* K-1s (without all 38 entry lines) so long as each item and amount reported follows the official format.

A Simple Trust Example

Now that you have some idea of what goes on a K-1, let's give an example of how K-1s are frequently used. For this purpose, consider a simple family trust. Assume that there are three beneficiaries whose designated allocable shares are A: 50%, B: 30%, and C: 20%. Also, assume that all administrative expense deductions are shared proportionately by all sources of trust income. Being a simple trust, there is no charitable deduction nor any property-in-kind distribution.

Many simple trusts have rental real estate as their primary income-producing asset. Such asset may consist of residential rentals, commercial rentals, industrial rentals, farmland rentals, or some combination thereof. Real estate, when properly managed, is durable and long lasting. It has the potential for appreciation when the trust is ready for termination.

With the above in mind, consider the following illustrative scenario of trust income and administrative expenses:

Interest	$ 1,000
Dividends	3,000
Capital gain	5,000
Net rents	36,000

Sched. K-1 (Form 1041)	BENEFICIARY'S SHARE OF INCOME, ETC.		Year
Name of Trust:			☐ Amended ☐ Final
Beneficiary's Tax ID		Trust's Tax ID	
BENEFICIARY Name & Address		FIDUCIARY Name & Address	
(a) Allocable Share Item		(b) Amount	(C) Enter Col.(b) on:
• Interest • Dividends _6 lines_ • Cap. gains			
• Annuities • Rents _8 lines_ • Royalties • Trade or business			
• Adjustments _3 lines_			
• Deductions _2 lines_			
• Tax preferences _4 lines_ • Exclusion items			
• Final year items • Unused deductions _7 lines_ • Loss carryovers			
Other (itemize) _8 lines_		XXXXXXXXXXXXXXXX	
a. • Payment credits b. • Tax-exempt interest c. _ _ _ _ _ _ _ _ _ _ _ _ _ d. _ _ _ _ _ _ _ _ _ _ _ _ _ e. _ _ _ _ _ _ _ _ _ _ _ _ _ f. _ _ _ _ _ _ _ _ _ _ _ _ _ g. _ _ _ _ _ _ _ _ _ _ _ _ _ h. _ _ _ _ _ _ _ _ _ _ _ _ _			

Fig. 12.5 - General Format of Schedule K-1 (Form 1040)

Total income	45,000
Administrative expense	<u><5,000></u>
Net amount to be distributed	$40,000

What is the "proper way" to prepare each beneficiary's K-1?

The proper way is to go through the detailed allocation procedure that we outline for you in Figure 12.6. Believe us; we have used income and expense amounts in simple rounded numbers. Unround the numbers and increase the number of income sources and/or the number of beneficiaries. Then watch simplicity become complexity.

STEP 1	Allocating the Character of Income			
	Class of Income	Amount	Allocation Fraction	Allocated Amount
1	Interest	$ 1,000	0.0222	$ 888
2	Dividends	3,000	0.0666	2,664
3	Cap. gain	5,000	0.1112	4,448
4	Net rents	36,000	0.800	32,000
	TOTALS	45,000	1.0000	40,000
	LESS All Administrative Deductions	< 5,000>		↑
	NET AMOUNT DISTRIBUTABLE	40,000		

XXXXXXXXXXXXXXXXXXXXXXXXXXXXXXXXXXXXXXXXXXXXXXXXXXXXX

STEP 2	Assignment to Designated Beneficiaries		
	Distributable Amount	A : 50%	B : 30%	C : 20%
1	888	444	266	178
2	2,664	1,332	800	532
3	4,448	2,224	1,334	890
4	32,000	16,000	9,600	6,400
	40,000	20,000	12,000	8,000

Fig. 12.6 - Worksheet for Allocating Currently Distributable Income

Other Simple K-1 Uses

The last category of items on Schedule K-1 is the grouping designated: *Other (itemize)*. There are eight entry lines there, (a) through (h). The first two have preprinted designations, namely: (a) credit for prepaid taxes, and (b) tax-exempt interest. The other six are blank. The blank lines are designated (c) through (h); they provide opportunities for distributing various forms of nontaxable money and property to the beneficiaries. A simple trust can use these lines, once all of its current (taxable) income is assigned to the beneficiaries who, in turn, report that income on their respective Forms 1040.

Our position is that any trust whose total assets are less than $3,000,000 (3 million) should be structured as a simple trust only. Also, the trust should be structured to terminate in 25 years or less, without any accumulations of current income or any contributions to charity. A competent and responsible trustee can easily — and prudently — distribute $3,000,000 over a 25-year period. On average, that would be $120,000 per year (120,000/yr x 25 yrs = 3,000,000). Depending on the special needs of different beneficiaries, some years might distribute more; other years less.

With the above in mind, let us postulate another scenario for using the K-1 in a simplified manner. The trust assets have been prudently managed, resulting in the following items being available for distribution:

(b)	Tax-exempt interest	$ 38,000
(c)	Depreciation reserve	30,000
(d)	Depletion reserve	20,000
(e)	Amortization reserve	10,000
(f)	Money market cash	25,000
(g)	Nontaxable annuity proceeds	15,000
(h)	Return of capital from sales	12,000
		$150,000

When any of these items are distributed to beneficiaries, the allocable share distributable amounts are **not taxable** to the recipients. Yes, this statement is correct! Every beneficiary loves to receive nontaxable distributions. This fact should be highlighted in the *Other (itemize)* portion of the K-1 by the typed or hand printed notation: NONTAXABLE; SEE ATTACHED. Then an explanation should be prepared as to why the item amounts listed are not taxed, and that they should not be reported on Form 1040.

Complex Trusts & Charities

There is no way that a complex trust can accomplish the simplicity of the K-1 items above. This is because such a trust involves complex issues, set-asides, and distribution options. The complications arise strictly from the accumulations of income and distributions of corpus property for special purposes, such as:

(1) the attainment of a specified age by beneficiaries who are minors or young adults;
(2) special care needs for disabled or elderly beneficiaries;
(3) deaths of successive beneficiaries;
(4) provisions for generation-skipping transfers; and
(5) contributions to charity and charitable remainders.

Whereas a simple trust may display two or three taxable entries on a K-1, a complex trust may have five to seven such entries. These additional entries imply three things. One, greater trust assets, perhaps considerably more than $3,000,000. Two, greater discretionary options and management skills by the trustee. And, three, greater tax sophistication by the beneficiaries and/or by the preparers of their 1040 returns.

Having greater assets means the generation of greater dividends and capital gains; greater passive income from real estate holdings; greater participation in active business enterprises (including farming); and a greater desire to contribute to charity.

Many creators of complex trusts are fascinated with "charitable remainder" features. Charitable remainder trusts (called: CRTs) are exempt from tax on the accumulated earnings of the trust . . . PROVIDED that all remainder interests — both income and corpus — go exclusively to charity. Additionally, the life expectancy for which the charitable remainder interests are computed is based on no more than two living beneficiaries. The noncharitable beneficiary(ies) must receive no less than 5% of the trust assets annually . . . and be taxed on them. When the survivor deceases, what's left goes to charity. Recall out discourse in Chapter 6 on Charitable Remainder Trusts.

Not every family trust arrangement is enamored with the charitable remainder concept. Many beneficiaries prefer the noncash property remnants themselves. Provisions in the trust instrument can address these preferences if all charitable remainder mandates are excluded. If the instrument so provides, IRC Section 643(e): *Treatment of Property Distributed in Kind*, comes into play.

Skip Persons & GST Tax

Generation-Skipping Trusts are quite common for families of modest and above-modest wealth providing for grandchildren, great-grandchildren, etc. These distributees of trust property are classed as: *skip persons*. Such persons are expressly defined in Section 2613(a)(1) as—

A natural person assigned to a generation which is 2 or more generations below the generation assignment of the transferor [trustor or grantor].

As explained in Chapter 9, the GST exemption of $1,000,000+ per trustor is allocated among the various skip persons, by name, description of property, and estate value. This is done on **Schedule R** of Form 706: *Generation-Skipping Transfer Tax*. A copy of Schedule R (as prepared for the trustor's estate) is required documentation for recordkeeping by the trustee of the GST trust.

When the time comes for the GST trustee to distribute property to a skip person in excess of that person's Schedule R (706) allocated exemption amount, the GST tax applies. As per Section 2621(a), this aspect of trust operation is called a *taxable distribution*. It is a TRANSFER TAX distribution: not an income tax distribution. Accordingly, Schedule K-1 (1041) would not apply. However, for informational purposes, a notation in the blank lines on Schedule K-1 at *Other (itemize)*, that a "Section 2621 distribution" had been made is well advised.

The substance of Section 2621: *Taxable Amount in Case of Taxable Distribution*, is that the GST tax is borne by the distributed property itself. As a prelude to the tax, the trustee prepares Form 706-GS(D-1): *Notification of Distribution from a Generation-Skipping Trust*. The GS(D-1) states the "inclusion ratio" and the market value of the property at the time of its distribution. Then the skip person distributee computes and pays the tax on Form 706-GS(D): *Generation-Skipping Transfer Tax for Distributions*. In the computational process, the distributee gets deductions for allowable expenses and any applicable state GST tax.

In the case of a final or termination distribution of property to a skip person, Form 706-GS(T) is used. This form is titled: *Generation-Skipping Transfer Tax Return for Terminations*. This form is prepared by the trustee and the tax is computed thereon. The termination amount to the distributee has had the GST tax and expenses taken out. That termination distributee is no longer a beneficiary of the trust.

As is often the case, a generation-skipping trust can be formulated so that the trust itself terminates when the last skip person receives his/her corpus share. Preferably, the termination should take place no later than 50 years after the last surviving trustor dies. Family trusts that go on for longer periods attract abusive inroads by egregious professionals, distant relatives, and investment con artists.

For families of truly significant wealth (say, well over $100,000,000), terminating their trust in 50 years is too short. They want their hereditary lines to go on and on. To achieve this longevity, a Private Foundation — rather than a family trust — may be the better way to go.

ABOUT

THE AUTHOR

Holmes F. Crouch

Born on a small farm in southern Maryland, Holmes was graduated from the U.S. Coast Guard Academy with a Bachelor's Degree in Marine Engineering. While serving on active duty, he wrote many technical articles on maritime matters. After attaining the rank of Lieutenant Commander, he resigned to pursue a career as a nuclear engineer.

Continuing his education, he earned a Master's Degree in Nuclear Engineering from the University of California. He also authored two books on nuclear propulsion. As a result of the tax write-offs associated with writing these books, the IRS audited his returns. The IRS's handling of the audit procedure so annoyed Holmes that he undertook to become as knowledgeable as possible regarding tax procedures. He became a licensed private Tax Practitioner by passing an examination administered by the IRS. Having attained this credential, he started his own tax preparation and counseling business in 1972.

In the early years of his tax practice, he was a regular talk-show guest on San Francisco's KGO Radio responding to hundreds of phone-in tax questions from listeners. He was a much sought-after guest speaker at many business seminars and taxpayer meetings. He also provided counseling on special tax problems, such as divorce matters, property exchanges, timber harvesting, mining ventures, animal breeding, independent contractors, selling businesses, and offices-at-home. Over the past 25 years, he has prepared well over 10,000 tax returns for individuals, estates, trusts, and small businesses (in partnership and corporate form).

During the tax season of January through April, he prepares returns in a unique manner. During a single meeting, he completes the return . . . *on the spot!* The client leaves with his return signed, sealed, and in a stamped envelope. His unique approach to preparing returns and his personal interest in his clients' tax affairs have honed his professional proficiency. His expertise extends through itemized deductions, computer-matching of income sources, capital gains and losses, business expenses and cost of goods, residential rental expenses, limited and general partnership activities, closely-held corporations, to family farms and ranches.

He remembers spending 12 straight hours completing a doctor's complex return. The next year, the doctor, having moved away, utilized a large accounting firm to prepare his return. Their accountant was so impressed by the manner in which the prior return was prepared that he recommended the doctor travel the 500 miles each year to have Holmes continue doing it.

He recalls preparing a return for an unemployed welder, for which he charged no fee. Two years later the welder came back and had his return prepared. He paid the regular fee . . . and then added a $300 tip.

During the off season, he represents clients at IRS audits and appeals. In one case a shoe salesman's audit was scheduled to last three hours. However, after examining Holmes' documentation it was concluded in 15 minutes with "no change" to his return. In another instance he went to an audit of a custom jeweler that the IRS dragged out for more than six hours. But, supported by Holmes' documentation, the client's return was accepted by the IRS with "no change."

Then there was the audit of a language translator that lasted two full days. The auditor scrutinized more than $1.25 million in gross receipts, all direct costs, and operating expenses. Even though all expensed items were documented and verified, the auditor decided that more than $23,000 of expenses ought to be listed as capital items for depreciation instead. If this had been enforced it would have resulted in a significant additional amount of tax. Holmes strongly disagreed and after many hours of explanation got the amount reduced by more than 60% on behalf of his client.

He has dealt extensively with gift, death and trust tax returns. These preparations have involved him in the tax aspects of wills, estate planning, trustee duties, probate, marital and charitable bequests, gift and death exemptions, and property titling.

Although not an attorney, he prepares Petitions to the U.S. Tax Court for clients. He details the IRS errors and taxpayer facts by citing pertinent sections of tax law and regulations. In a recent case involving an attorney's ex-spouse, the IRS asserted a tax deficiency of $155,000. On behalf of his client, he petitioned the Tax Court and within six months the IRS conceded the case.

Over the years, Holmes has observed that the IRS is not the industrious, impartial, and competent federal agency that its official public imaging would have us believe.

He found that, at times, under the slightest pretext, the IRS has interpreted against a taxpayer in order to assess maximum penalties, and may even delay pending matters so as to increase interest due on additional taxes. He has confronted the IRS in his own behalf on five separate occasions, going before the U.S. Claims Court, U.S. District Court, and U.S. Tax Court. These were court actions that tested specific sections of the Internal Revenue Code which he found ambiguous, inequitable, and abusively interpreted by the IRS.

Disturbed by the conduct of the IRS and by the general lack of tax knowledge by most individuals, he began an innovative series of taxpayer-oriented Federal tax guides. To fulfill this need, he undertook the writing of a series of guidebooks that provide in-depth knowledge on one tax subject at a time. He focuses on subjects that plague taxpayers all throughout the year. Hence, his formulation of the "Allyear" Tax Guide series.

The author is indebted to his wife, Irma Jean, and daughter, Barbara MacRae, for the word processing and computer graphics that turn his experiences into the reality of these publications. Holmes welcomes comments, questions, and suggestions from his readers. He can be contacted in California at (408) 867-2628, or by writing to the publisher's address.

ALLYEAR Tax Guides
by Holmes F. Crouch

Series 100 - INDIVIDUALS AND FAMILIES

BEING SELF-EMPLOYED .... T/G 101
DEDUCTING JOB EXPENSES .... T/G 102
FAMILY TAX STRATEGIES .... T/G 103
RESOLVING DIVORCE ISSUES .... T/G 104
CITIZENS WORKING ABROAD .... T/G 105

Series 200 - INVESTORS AND BUSINESSES

INVESTOR GAINS & LOSSES .... T/G 201
SIDE BUSINESS VENTURES .... T/G 202
STARTING YOUR BUSINESS .... T/G 203
MAKING PARTNERSHIPS WORK .... T/G 204
SMALL C & S CORPORATIONS.......................... T/G 205

Series 300 - RETIREES AND ESTATES

DECISIONS WHEN RETIRING .... T/G 301
WRITING YOUR WILL .... T/G 302
SIMPLIFYING YOUR ESTATE .... T/G 303
YOUR EXECUTOR DUTIES .... T/G 304
YOUR TRUSTEE DUTIES .... T/G 305

Series 400 - OWNERS AND SELLERS

RENTAL REAL ESTATE .... T/G 401
OWNING NATURAL RESOURCES .... T/G 402
FAMILY TRUSTS & TRUSTORS.......................... T/G 403
SELLING YOUR HOME(S) .... T/G 404
SELLING YOUR BUSINESS .... T/G 405

Series 500 - AUDITS AND APPEALS

KEEPING GOOD RECORDS .... T/G 501
WINNING YOUR AUDIT............................... T/G 502
DISAGREEING WITH THE IRS .... T/G 503
CONTESTING IRS PENALTIES .... T/G 504
GOING INTO TAX COURT .... T/G 505

For information about the above titles,
and/or a free 8 page catalog, contact:

www.allyeartax.com
Phone: (408) 867-2628   Fax: (408) 867-6466